The ⬛⬛
Expe⬛⬛

A PLAY ⬛⬛⬛

BY

NAUNTON DAVIES

AUTHOR OF

"The Human Factor," "The Second Son," "The
Schemer," "Daughters of Eve," etc., "The Cobweb"
and "The Wanton" (in collaboration with Leon
M. Lion), etc., etc.

AND

STANLEY DREWITT

NOTE.—The features of this play were outlined before
the outbreak of the great war, which has verified
many of the ideas of the Authors, and converted
what were prophetic propositions into facts.

ACT I.

SCENE I.—A Room in Wenallt Castle.

SCENE II.—Shop and Store-room, Jenkin Lewis' Factory.

ACT II.

A Week Later.

SCENE I.—Outside White Barn.

SCENE II.—The Library at Wenallt Castle.

ACT III.

Two Years Later.

SCENE : The same as in Act I.

ACT IV.

Six Months Later.

SCENE : The same as in Act II.

Time : Present Day.

Locality : Carmarthenshire.

CHARACTERS :

LLEWELYN GARTH	Jacob Morgan's adopted son.
RODERICK WENALLT, M.P.	Lord Wenallt's nephew and supposed heir.
LADY VIOLET WENALLT	Of Wenallt Castle : distantly related to Lord Wenallt.
LORD WENALLT	Cabinet Minister Violet's Guardian.
JENKIN LEWIS	Factory Owner.
JACOB MORGAN	Shop-keeper.
ARLAIS LEWIS, B.A.	Jenkin Lewis' daughter.
LADY WENALLT	The Minister's wife.
WILKIN WATKINS	An eccentric M.P.
MATTHEW JONES	Foreman at Jenkin Lewis' Factory.
ROGERS and Another	Game-keepers to Roderick Wenallt.
DAVIE	A Servant.
TOM " SAIS " (English Tom)	Workman at the Factory.
WILLIAMS	Footman at Wenallt Castle.

The Great Experiment

ACT I.

SCENE I.   *A room in Wenallt Castle.   Afternoon.*

As the curtain rises, the footman, WILLIAMS, *ushers in* JACOB MORGAN, *who is a benevolent-looking round-faced, clean-shaven man, with a twinkle in his shrewd eyes, about* 60, *and wears a suit of Welsh " home-spun."*

FOOTMAN (*placing chair*) : **If you'll take a seat, Mr. Morgan, I'll tell his lordship that you are here.**
(*Exit.*)

JACOB MORGAN *sits down, takes up a newspaper, tries to read, but his eyes wander round restlessly, and he throws down the paper, gets up and fidgets until* LORD WENALLT *comes in.*

LORD WENALLT *is an intellectual looking man, with a fine face and head, thoughtful, observant eyes, about* 60. *Good nature and strong character mark his expression, which is kindly, whimsical, and determined by turns.*

LORD WENALLT (*with a pleasant smile*) : **Good morning, Jacob. What brings you here ? Is Garth in trouble again ?**

JACOB MORGAN : No, my lord——he's never in trouble of his own making.

7

LORD WENALLT : You are loyal. One would think he was your own son, and not the child of unknown parents—a nameless boy.

JACOB MORGAN : A boy? You forget, my lord, that it's twenty-five years since you brought him to me, when he was no bigger than that. (*Holds his hand to indicate the height of a child of three or four.*)

LORD WENALLT (*reflectively*) : **Twenty-five** years ago ! Is it so long? (*Glances at a painting of a child hung on the wall.*)

JACOB MORGAN : And for twenty-five years I've been wondering who he is. It's hard that he should have only a borrowed name—very hard. Ill-natured people throw it in his face, and I don't like it.

LORD WENALLT : He is your adopted son ; that should protect him. A foundling, even, should have as much respect paid to him as a man with a pedigree. Why do they do it?

JACOB MORGAN : Because he is above them in mind and body ; because he is making his way in the world against odds that would daunt most men ; because he overshadows their littleness, and because it's the way of small natures to pull great natures down. And now, because the election is coming on, and Garth isn't on the side of either Party, Mr. Wenallt is up against him, and pelts him

8

with mud, and whispers about that he's a stray from Australia. (*Sternly*) I won't have it, my lord.

LORD WENALLT : I must speak to my nephew about it. Do you know why he's taken such a dislike to Garth ?

JACOB MORGAN : Garth is too popular to please him, and he's got the courage to have views of his own, and to denounce the dishonesty of the Party System. And there's another reason : Lady Violet sometimes takes Garth's side in the village meetings, and that makes Mr. Wenallt wild.

LORD WENALLT : Naturally—she is to be Mr. Wenallt's wife. He expects her to support him.

JACOB MORGAN : But Garth can't help that.

LORD WENALLT (*thoughtfully*) : No, of course not. It has made things rather difficult, I'm afraid.

JACOB MORGAN (*with a scoff*) : Difficult ? What is a little difficulty compared to the insults Garth's got to stand ? (*Impetuously*) I won't see him put upon by the biggest gentleman in the land ; and, if I tell the truth, Mr. Roderick Wenallt isn't fit to lace his boots.

LORD WENALLT : You are very severe on my nephew, my friend. He's merely following the instincts of his class, and offering the world the fruits—such as they are—of his upbringing.

JACOB MORGAN : I can't help that (*walks about, fuming*). He has roused the devil in me,

9

and it's my Welsh temper is speaking. I would rather go back to Australia, and take Garth with me, than stand such insolence.

LORD WENALLT : Garth would want a lot of taking, I think. From all I've heard, I should say he isn't the sort to run away from the sound of the guns.

JACOB MORGAN (*hotly*) : Not 'till he's given Mr. Wenallt a down-right good hiding.

LORD WENALLT : It might do him good, certainly. But you must forego that amusement for the present, Jacob.—Who knows ? Perhaps destiny has marked out Garth's course for him. If so, no sentiment of yours nor sympathy of mine ought to be allowed to come between him and his future.

JACOB MORGAN (*indignantly*) : His future ! What I'm concerned about is his past. I want to know who he is, who his parents were, and why he's been kept in ignorance of his birth. (*Abruptly*) : Is he your son, my lord ?

LORD WENALLT (*startled for a moment by the abruptness of the question, quickly shakes off his surprise, and smiles good-naturedly*) : If he were my son he would be heir to my estates. Do you think I am the man to let such an important person run wild ? You must forgive me, old friend, if I can't tell you all you want to know. It might, if prematurely divulged, interfere with the success of a great

10

experiment which his father has at heart and has sacrificed much to attain.

JACOB MORGAN : What is this experiment you talk about, my lord ? If I knew something about it, I might feel more contented.

LORD WENALLT (*after a moment's thoughtful consideration*) : Yes—I think I can tell you that. Garth's father (*hesitates*)—is—is a friend of mine—a man of ideas, who started his public career with great political aspirations and clean-cut convictions. He believed in the honesty of Party Government and the power of Cabinets to grapple with the evils which check the progress of the human race. The blind struggling of the people—not of one section but of all—to attain the goal Nature has set before them, he watched with absorbed interest and anxious hope. He saw how progress was impeded by the clash of classes fostered by politicians for Party ends. Gradually, the failure of the Party System forced itself upon him. But why had it failed ?

JACOB MORGAN : Garth says it's because Cabinet Ministers live in a world of their own—a world above the every-day world, and that they get their ideas of outside things from a tainted source.

LORD WENALLT : From a tainted source ! What does he mean ?

JACOB MORGAN : Well, he means paid politicians, who think with one eye on their pockets, and

11

the other on a dissolution, and never give a thought to what is right, but only to what is expedient.

LORD WENALLT : It's an uncompromising indictment ! But he may be right, and, if he is, it is a justification of his father's experiment. How has he found out these things ?

JACOB MORGAN : He is one of the people ; he is in the fight ; and realises the condition of the struggle.

LORD WENALLT : Ah ! it is true ! Yes—to understand the people, you must be of them. You must begin at the foundation, and build storey by storey, until you reach the top. Then the people may cry in their hearts : " This is mine. I helped to build it !" It would be the union of the classes, realised through the knowledge that the efforts of all are needed to complete the national edifice. I begin to see what a wonderful world it would be if the factions, which are now pulling against each other in the same boat, could be united by a compelling Idea, and made to pull together.

JACOB MORGAN : That is what Garth is hoping for. But he is young and enthusiastic. At the same time, he owns it can't be done, until some great Statesman, rising above Party interests, can reach the heart of the people and carry them with him.

LORD WENALLT : And that is so difficult for a Cabinet Minister. He is merely a bit of the mechanism in the Party machine, always under suspicion, and has no real liberty, no human link to bridge the gulf between himself and those he would serve. Perhaps it was that conviction that induced Garth's father to send this boy of his out into the world— this boy without a name, stript of repelling wealth and position—to dwell amongst the people, and grow up in their atmosphere, so that, in the course of time, he might return from his fight with the world, ripe with the knowledge of the needs of his fellowmen, to be the eyes and the ears and inspiration of his father.

JACOB MORGAN (*with emotion*) : My lord, I think I understand. If I could tell Garth what you have said, it would go to his heart, as it has gone to mine, and comfort him. It is a great idea ; and there is a high example behind it. God Himself sent His Son into the world to see and to suffer and to teach. It was the only way to reach the hearts of the Unbelievers, and get them to listen and believe. (*Drops his voice—feelingly*) : And Garth has suffered. I have been true to my promise, and let him fight his own battles unhelped—except for a word of encouragement now and then.

LORD WENALLT : Without suffering, there's no understanding. It was part of the experiment that he should share the work, the hardships, the rewards, and the hopes of the multitude.

JACOB MORGAN : I think he can claim that he has done something to help them to look over the mountain tops and see the things beyond, and shown them that it is better to climb the mountain than try to pull it down.

LORD WENALLT : Ah ! then the sacrifice has not been for nothing. There was always the risk that the boy might go under in the fight, and lose his personality. But his father believed in heredity, believed in the ordered instincts of generations of Statesmen, and felt that they must modify in his son the disorderly tendencies of the times. (*A pause.*) When the harvest is fit for garnering, Jacob, you will find that I shall be one of the reapers.

JACOB MORGAN (*appealingly*) : It goes to my heart to see him fighting in the dark like this. Let me tell him just a few words to encourage him. (LORD WENALLT *shakes his head.*) I beg of you, my lord !

LORD WENALLT (*dropping his hand kindly on* JACOB'S *shoulder and looking him in the eyes with a smile*) : Not just yet, old friend. After all these years you must trust me a little longer.

(LADY VIOLET *comes in quickly, with a bright smile, in walking costume, and runs up to* JACOB MORGAN. *She is a distinguished looking girl, about 20, with a sweet face and eyes that hold the memory.*)

LADY VIOLET : Good morning, Mr. Morgan

14

(*shakes hands impulsively*). Why didn't you tell me you were here? You know how I love to gossip with you.

JACOB MORGAN : Well, you see, Lady Violet, I left all my gossip at home to-day, and didn't like meeting you with an empty budget.

LADY VIOLET : Budget ! horrid word ! I'm just going down to Jenkin Lewis' factory with Roderick, on a political mission. Sounds big, doesn't it ? (*Laughs.*)

LORD WENALLT : What are you going there for ?

LADY VIOLET : To ask Mr. Lewis for his vote for Roderick.

LORD WENALLT (*smiling*) : Still beating the Party drum, child, are you ?

LADY VIOLET : No, most noble guardian. Roderick beats the drum, and I gossip with the villagers. They are dears, and I love to gossip with them, and drink tea out of their old china, and—and—oh ! lots of things.

LORD WENALLT : Rank bribery !

JACOB MORGAN : It's the right way to win elections, Lady Violet. Go amongst them, be of them, and don't look down upon them from heights they can never reach. It makes them sceptical and hard.

LORD WENALLT : Do you do it for fun, or because you feel an interest in the villagers ? (*Watches her intently.*)

LADY VIOLET (*suddenly serious—and a little reproachful*): How can you ask me such a question?

LORD WENALLT (*gravely*): I beg your pardon, my dear. I wouldn't hurt your feelings for the world, and I know you wouldn't hurt theirs. You form a link between the Castle and the Cottage, and are equally at home in both. That is how it should be. How do you do it?

LADY VIOLET : Can't you guess, you dear old thing ?

LORD WENALLT (*shakes his head*) : No.

LADY VIOLET (*with a bright laugh*): Nor can I ! (*going.*)

LORD WENALLT (*looks after her with a smile as she runs out*): Ah ! That's why she succeeds. (*Thoughtfully.*) I should like to see Garth. You must tell him to come up here to talk to me. He may teach a Cabinet Minister, who is a mere student in human affairs, many things he is ignorant about (*glances up at the picture on the wall*).

END OF SCENE.

16

ACT I.

The same day—later.

Scene II : *A large room in Jenkin Lewis' Factory. At the back there is a shop window, divided by a central door, looking out on to a road in the village. Part of the room is used as an office. A desk, table, and chairs, counters and shelves, laden with stocks of flannels and tweeds, and an ancient Grandfather's clock, complete the furniture. There is a door leading into the shop parlour.*

Jenkin Lewis, *the proprietor, is seated at the table. In front of him there is a box containing money and his workmen's pay sheets. He appears to be a well-to-do man of 50, with a sharp, obstinate face, and keen restless eyes. Scattered about the room, some seated on boxes and chairs, others standing, there are about a dozen of his workmen, whom he is paying.*

JENKIN LEWIS (*sharply*) : More pay and less work—that is what you want.

MATTHEW JONES : And you 'ould want it, too, if you was in our place.

JENKIN LEWIS : You don't earn what I am giving you.

MATTHEW JONES : That is a lie, Mr. Lewis ; and I 'on't take it from you or anybody else.

LLEWELYN GARTH *comes in quickly through the shop door. He is a striking-looking young man, about 30, with a handsome, thoughtful face and well-set-up figure. Dressed in a dark-blue lounge suit, he looks a fine type of our English or Welsh middle-class, and has about him that indefinable something which is called personality.*

(*A slight pause.*)

JENKIN LEWIS : Don't you talk to me like that ! I'm telling you the truth.

MATTHEW JONES (*defiantly*) : Well, tell it to Mr. Garth here. He'll tell you the same.

JENKIN LEWIS : Yes, I will tell him (*pauses and shuffles the papers about the table.*)

LLEWELYN GARTH : What is it, Mr. Lewis ?

MATTHEW JONES : We are asking for a rise, and he answers us that we don't earn what we are getting.

JENKIN LEWIS : And you don't earn it—not one of you.

LLEWELYN GARTH : Oh ? Surely, you don't accuse your old workmen—your neighbours and dependents for many years—of obtaining money by false pretences ?

JENKIN LEWIS : I never said that !

MATTHEW JONES (*warmly*) : Yes, you did.

LLEWELYN GARTH : Sit down, Matthew. You can't settle a dispute by heaping coals of fire on each

18

other. Let us talk it over quietly. We are all friends, and it's only fools that quarrel.

JENKIN LEWIS (*hotly*) : I am a peaceable man, and, what is more (*striking the table violently with his hand*), a reasonable man, and always for the right. But it is not right to give them a rise when they don't earn it. What do they want more money for ?

MATTHEW *jumps to his feet—an angry retort on his lips.*

LLEWELYN GARTH : I'll tell him, Matthew. (MATTHEW *sits down.*) We all want more money, Mr. Lewis ; it is a human weakness. You want it because it gives you more power, places you higher in the social scale, and brings nearer the day when you can write J.P. after your name. The workmen want it to furnish their cottages more comfortably, to enable their wives and children to have better food and better clothes, and spare moments to cultivate their minds and stand up in the face of the sun and claim a little of the warmth that God made for all men.

JENKIN LEWIS : Are you preaching a sermon ?

LLEWELYN GARTH (*smiling*) : No ; I'm just chatting about a worldly matter.

JENKIN LEWIS : Then, why do you bring God into it ?

LLEWELYN GARTH : I thought it would appeal

to your Celtic soul. But, as you object to God, and claim all the sun for yourself————

JENKIN LEWIS : I am a God-fearing man.

LLEWELYN GARTH : It is just ambition, and nothing else, that possesses you and your workmen. If it comes to a fair trial between you, their claim to better wages is stronger than yours to bigger profits.

MATTHEW JONES : Hear ! hear !

JENKIN LEWIS (*rising, and looking over his spectacles at* GARTH) : Llewelyn Garth ! If you don't mind what you are about your unnatural flow of language will lead you into Parliament—or the Asylum. Because you have got a B.A. after your name, and do my accounts, you think I want J.P. after my name, do you ?

MATTHEW JONES : It is common talk, whatever.

JACOB MORGAN *looks in at the shop door. He has a fishing basket slung over his shoulder. Leaning on his fishing rod, just inside the door, he listens to the conversation with a whimsical smile, unobserved by the others.*

JENKIN LEWIS : Ah ! Jacob Morgan, I want to talk to you. You have been saying things about me and the J.P., have you ?

JACOB MORGAN : Well, you want the J.P., don't you ?

JENKIN LEWIS : If I had it, I 'ouldn't sit on the same bench as you.

JACOB MORGAN : You are too prosperous— that's what's the matter with you, friend Jenkin. They tell me you are making twenty per cent. on your workmen's labour.

MATTHEW JONES : Yes—and more.

JENKIN LEWIS : You know nothing about it.

JACOB MORGAN : Twenty per cent. on a bit of flannel ! It is a big profit. Spend a little of it on the men who are making it for you, friend Jenkin. You will find it more profitable in the end to buy a place in Heaven than a seat on the Bench.

JENKIN LEWIS (*furiously*) : You will make me lose my temper in a minute, and I am not going to lose it. It is not my habit.

LLEWELYN GARTH (*smiling*) : Come, Matthew, tell us exactly what you want.

MATTHEW JONES : We want a shilling a week rise all round.

JACOB MORGAN : Is that all ! Good gracious, Jenkin Lewis, I thought they wanted all you have got, and a little more, by the fuss you are making.

LLEWELYN GARTH : Trade is good, Mr. Lewis. Let them have it.

JENKIN LEWIS : I will shut up the factory first.
The men jump to their feet, and murmur angrily.

LLEWELYN GARTH : Shut up the factory !
You don't mean that ?

JENKIN LEWIS : I am a man of my word.

LLEWLEYN GARTH : I can't believe it. Think
what it would mean to you and the men : misery
for them, perhaps ruin for you.

JENKIN LEWIS : Tell them to think. If I think
for ever, I can't make one sovereign into two.
To-day it is a shilling they want, and to-morrow it
will be two shillings. There is no reason in them.
(*Paces the room, his mind filled with bitter thoughts—
turns to the men sharply*) : For years I have fed and
clothed you, and my father before me did the same,
and, for thanks, you turn against me like
this.

WILKIN WATKIN *saunters up to the shop door,
and looks in curiously. Dressed in an old black
frock coat, with the cuffs turned up, and a ragged
cap, with the peak pulled over his ear, trousers
patched and much too long for him, and a pair of
unlaced sloppy shoes, he looks the picture of un-
tidiness and neglect. His age may be anything from
30 to 40 ; and the contented expression of his face
seems to indicate that his soul is somewhere laughing
in his body under his dilapidated exterior. He has
a habit of closing his eyes, masking an eccentric
shrewdness under the expression of utter blankness,
and chuckling to himself without apparent cause, as*

though he lived in a secret world peopled with creatures of his own fancy.

MATTHEW JONES : We are not turning against you.   We are trying to draw you to us.

JENKIN LEWIS (*passionately*) : You are trying to ruin me.   You 'ould take the coat off my back and the bread out of my mouth (*seizes a chair, and swings it out of his way*.).

JACOB MORGAN : You have got a devil of a temper, Jenkin Lewis.   You will have to be more calm if you ever get the J.P.

ONE OF THE MEN (*seeing* WILKIN) : Hullo ! Wilkin.

WILKIN WATKINS (*shambles in—in a sing-song voice, like a chant*) : Wilkin Watkins is my name, Wales is my nation—(*pauses, and looks with dull, wondering eyes at* JENKIN LEWIS ; *then breaks into a low gurgling laugh, turns to* MATTHEW, *and jerks his thumb towards* JENKIN LEWIS) : In a temper, is he ?

JENKIN LEWIS (*suddenly turning upon* WILKIN) : What are you doing here, you Godless vagabond ?

WILKIN WATKINS : Hullo ! Mr. Lewis.   You are alive, are you ?   You are barking grand.   You make me feel quite joyful.   (*Chants*) : O ! let us be joyful—joyful, joyful, joy-oy-ful !

JENKIN LEWIS (*sternly*) : I am asking what are you doing here ?

WILKIN WATKINS : To be truthful, I was singing just this minute. (*Chants*) : **Down amongst the dead men.**—O ! let us be joyful. (*Chuckles.*) They was saying in the village that you was dead. (*Chants.*)

> If you was dead and in your grave, and all your
>   bones was rotten—
> We'd see your ghost in this old place, when you
>   was quite forgotten.

A WORKMAN *shouts* " A-men! " *Cries of derision from the others.*

JENKIN LEWIS (*grimly*) : I am not dead, yet.

WILKIN WATKINS : No—the gods don't love you enough. I thought, perhaps, if it was true, I might have an old coat after you—something to remember you by. Better luck next time, Mr. Lewis (*chuckles*).

JENKIN LEWIS (*points to the door, B*) : Go away home.

WILKIN WATKINS : Thank you, indeed, Mr. Lewis, but I haven't got no home. Plenty of rain lately to keep the old wheel going, grinding and grinding, and making money for you. Give-and-take is your motto, Mr. Lewis : give all you have got, and take nothing back. And I am the same sort of fellow. Too soft-hearted I am. I am always ready to take a penny (*holds out his hand*) if a gentle-man can't give me tuppence (*chuckles*).

24

JENKIN LEWIS : Go home, I tell you.

WILKIN WATKINS (*seriously*) : Time for another funeral, isn't it, Mr. Lewis ? Chance for a drop of beer, then, and a bit of cake (*chuckles*). Make me feel quite jolly to think of it. They do say in the village that Mr. Roderick is after Lady Violet, and that he is going about the lanes with her—the same as he used to go about with Miss Lewis.

JENKIN LEWIS (*seizes* WILKIN *by the collar of his coat and shakes him*) : You wicked fool ! what lies are you telling about my daughter ?

WILKIN WATKINS : No lies, indeed to goodness !

JENKIN LEWIS : You have been drinking or you are dreaming.

WILKIN WATKINS : Dreaming I am, I am sure, because I had no money to get drink. Don't you trouble about my old stories—(*touches his head*). There is something odd inside my old head, and it do come out the wrong way up sometimes (*yawns as though very tired*). I am working for people, and don't get no wages, and no food half my time. Perhaps that is why my head is so empty.

WILKIN *curls himself up on a bale of goods in a corner of the shop, and appears to go to sleep : but he now and then raises his head, and shows that he is listening.*

RODERICK WENALLT, M.P., *and* LADY VIOLET WENALLT *come to the shop door, and pause for a moment, looking in. He is a well-groomed, dark-haired, pale-faced man of about 40-45, with an air of confidence—a cool man of the fashionable world, obviously a little cynical and patronising.*

LLEWELYN GARTH : Now, Mr. Lewis, won't you reconsider your decision ?

JENKIN LEWIS : I'll be glad to see your back, Llewelyn Garth.

MATTHEW JONES : Wait a bit ! If there's going to be any dismissing, you can dismiss the lot of us. Stand by us, Mr. Garth, and we'll stand by you.

RODERICK WENALLT *raps on the door with his stick to attract attention.*

JENKIN LEWIS (*without looking round*) : Come in !

RODERICK WENALLT (*coming in, with a smile*): I'm afraid I've called at an awkward moment, Mr. Lewis (*shakes hands with* JENKIN LEWIS, *nods casually to others*).

JENKIN LEWIS : Awkward enough, indeed, Mr. Wenallt. There is no satisfying these men whatever I do.

RODERICK WENALLT : I'm sorry to hear that (*they walk aside and converse together*).

LADY VIOLET (*crosses to* GARTH, *smiles and nods to* MATTHEW *and the* MEN, *who rise and greet her respectfully*) : What is it all about, Mr. Garth ? Is there any fresh trouble in the Factory ?

26

LLEWELYN GARTH : Just a little family quarrel, Lady Violet.

LADY VIOLET (*smiling*) : Is that a hint that it is no business of mine ?

LLEWELYN GARTH : Oh, no—I never meant that. The welfare of the villagers always lies near your heart, I know.

LADY VIOLET : Thank you for saying that.

ARLAIS LEWIS (*calling from the parlour*) : Father ! tea is ready.

RODERICK WENALLT (*listens—smiles to himself as though pleasantly surprised*) : Is that Miss Lewis ? I thought she was at Girton.

JENKIN LEWIS : She is at home. I wasn't aware that you knew my daughter.

RODERICK WENALLT : My dear Mr. Lewis, I guessed that it was your daughter from her voice : it's so remarkably like yours.

JENKIN LEWIS : Yes, to be sure. There are great singers in our family.

RODERICK WENALLT : Ah ! I understood you were a fine singer. I expect you have won many prizes at the Eisteddfod ?

LADY VIOLET : Oh, Roderick !

WILKIN WATKINS (*slouching forward*) : Good-now ! Mr. Wenallt, you haven't got much of a ear for music. Mr. Lewis got a voice like a raven ; and Miss Arlais can sing like a nightingale. But,

27

perhaps, you haven't heard her sing about the lanes in the moonlight ?

RODERICK WENALLT *stares contemptuously at* WILKIN *through his eye-glass.*

ARLAIS LEWIS (*steps brightly into the room, with a smile on her lips*) : Dad ! (*She sees* RODERICK WENALLT.) Oh ! I didn't know you had visitors. (*A covert glance of recognition passes between her and* RODERICK WENALLT.)

She is a bright, attractive girl, about the same age as LADY VIOLET, *with a refined, pretty face, and dainty manners, and dainty shoes. She wears a becoming frock of artistic Welsh flannel, which sets off a remarkably graceful figure to great advantage. A typical Welsh girl, with Girton culture.*

RODERICK WENALLT : I should like to know your daughter, Mr. Lewis, if you will introduce me.

WILKIN WATKINS (*to himself*) : Well, I'm——! O ! let us be joyful ! (*turns away chuckling*).

JENKIN LEWIS (*ungraciously*) : Arlais, this is Mr. Roderick Wenallt, our member (*watches* RODERICK WENALLT *suspiciously*).

ARLAIS LEWIS : Yes, I know—(RODERICK WENALLT *gives her a warning glance*)—at least, I have heard of Mr. Wenallt, of course. His name is often in the papers.

RODERICK WENALLT : I have often wished to know you, Miss Lewis. Will you do me a favour ?

28

ARLAIS LEWIS (*a little surprised*) : If I can,
I will.

RODERICK WENALLT (*with distant courtesy*) :
Thank you, Miss Lewis.   You probably don't know
that I am canvassing for the coming election, and
want your father's support ?

ARLAIS LEWIS : Oh, yes, I know that.   You
have always voted for a Wenallt, haven't you,
father ?

JENKIN LEWIS : That's no reason why I should
go on doing it, is it ?

ARLAIS LEWIS : Yes, the best reason in the
world—if you wish to be consistent and true to those
who are true to you.

LADY VIOLET : You have a warm advocate in
Miss Lewis, Roderick.   I hope you will justify her
championship.   (*Coming towards* ARLAIS) : I hope
you haven't forgotten me, Arlais ?

ARLAIS LEWIS (*takes* LADY VIOLET'S *proferred
hand*) : Oh, no, indeed, Lady Violet.

LADY VIOLET (*laughingly*) : I thought, perhaps,
now that you are a Girton girl, flushed with honours,
and a B.A., you might soar into the clouds and look
down upon poor country folk.

ARLAIS LEWIS : Please—please don't think me
so stupid, Lady Violet.

LADY VIOLET : My dear girl, I think you are
just splendid.   You ought to be proud of your daugh-

ter, Mr. Lewis. I'm sure you'll find her a great comfort to you.

JENKIN LEWIS : I don't know. Young people are all for amusement and going away from home these days.

RODERICK WENALLT : Quite right, too. A clever girl like your daughter can't be expected to bury herself alive in a place like this. Women are coming into their kingdom ; and man's selfishness mustn't stand in their way. Intellect and education will assert themselves, Mr. Lewis, in spite of us.

LLEWELYN GARTH : Isn't there something more than intellect and education needed to found a woman's kingdom, Mr. Wenallt ?

RODERICK WENALLT (*with thinly veiled sarcasm*) : Oh, of course, it should be a place where the sun always shines, and the birds sing, and where men bow down in reverence before a petticoat, and think no evil.

RODERICK WENALLT *takes* ARLAIS *aside, and converses with her in low tones.* GARTH *talks earnestly with* MATTHEW *and the* MEN.

JACOB MORGAN (*taking roses from his fishing basket*) : The sun shines for a plucked flower, but the flower withers, Mr. Wenallt. Remember that, when you are saying your smart things. Something told me I should see you to-day, Lady Violet (*offers rose*).

30

LADY VIOLET : You are always waylaying me with pretty presents (*pins rose in her frock*). It's a good thing you haven't a daughter of your own, or you'd be spending all your fortune upon her.

JACOB MORGAN, *strangely affected, turns away, and busies himself with his basket.*

ARLAIS LEWIS (*crosses to her father, coaxingly*) : Father, you will vote for Mr. Wenallt, won't you ?

LADY VIOLET : He is an excellent candidate. He will tell you so himself.

JENKIN LEWIS : I think you had better go and see about the tea, Arlais.

ARLAIS LEWIS : Oh ! (*smiles at* RODERICK WENALLT—*runs off, laughing—R.*).

RODERICK WENALLT (*to* LADY VIOLET) : Your recommendation is not likely to do me much good.

LADY VIOLET : You oughtn't to need a recommendation, and you wouldn't, if you lived more in the Constituency.

RODERICK WENALLT : I'll do that—when we set up housekeeping together.

LADY VIOLET (*with a sweet, disarming smile*) : Don't count on that, Cousin Roderick.

RODERICK WENALLT : Uncertainty is the sauce of pursuit.

LADY VIOLET : Really, I'm not a quarry for any sportsman to trap. Mr. Lewis, do promise to vote for him, and send him back to that stupid Parliament out of the way.

JENKIN LEWIS : There is no use sending him to Parliament, if he 'on't do something to stop strikes.

MATTHEW JONES : You are the man to stop strikes, Mr. Lewis.

RODERICK WENALLT : Send me back as your Representative, and I promise to deal with strikes with a firm hand.

LLEWELYN GARTH : A firm hand, Mr. Wenallt, may deal out justice or injustice. Which will yours deal out ? There are several voters here, and they would like to know.

RODERICK WENALLT : If they will do me the honour to attend my meetings they will be fully enlightened.

LLEWELYN GARTH : Why not enlighten them now ? Your views might help us to find a way out of our present difficulty.

RODERICK WENALLT : Ah, just so. But I must choose my own time. You may be sure that the men's legitimate interests——

LLEWELYN GARTH : What are their legitimate interests ?

RODERICK WENALLT : Whatever they are, they shall receive my most favourable consideration.

LLEWELYN GARTH : Platitudes are no use, Mr. Wenallt. We don't want to be drugged with political sedatives. They may soothe the nerves of the credulous, but they don't touch the cause of the disease. (*Turns away and converses with the* WORKMEN. LADY VIOLET *follows him, and joins in the conversation.*)

RODERICK WENALLT (*shrugs his shoulders*) : My views evidently do not appeal to Mr. Garth. I hope you won't desert me, Mr. Lewis ?

JENKIN LEWIS : I will make a bargain with you. Get your Party to pass a Bill to stop strikes, and I will do all I can for you. If you can't promise that, settle this dispute to my satisfaction——

Murmurs from the MEN.

MATTHEW JONES : Hold hard, Mr. Lewis ! We don't want outsiders to meddle between us, eh, boys ? (MEN *shout "No !"*).

RODERICK WENALLT (*to* JENKIN LEWIS) : I think that settles it—unless you have the courage to assert your right to a voice in your own business.

LADY VIOLET : If I were you, Mr. Lewis, I would ask Mr. Garth to do what is right between you and the men. I have been talking to them, and sympathise with their feelings. The men trust him, and will be satisfied if he decides against them. (*Turns to the* MEN) : Isn't that so ?

ONE OF THE MEN : Yes—yes, that's it.

MATTHEW JONES : Right, my lady ! He will be fair to both sides.

RODERICK WENALLT : My dear Violet, are you turning Socialist ? You ought to know that a master can hardly entrust his interests to a workman's advocate.

JENKIN LEWIS : I am not going to trust him.

LADY VIOLET (*reproachfully to* RODERICK WENALLT) : There ! you see what you have done.

RODERICK WENALLT : Everybody hasn't got the same faith in Mr. Garth's disinterestedness as you have. I don't blame him for sticking up for his class ; but you can't expect a man in his position to be fair to an employer.

LADY VIOLET : A fair man can be fair to everybody.

LLEWELYN GARTH : Mr. Wenallt wouldn't understand that. He has used the weapon of distrust too much to see beyond it. Mistrust is the curse of men who live too much for themselves, and have no thought to spare for their neighbours. Such men never do any good : suspicion makes them cynical and—useless.

RODERICK WENALLT : What do you mean ?

LLEWELYN GARTH : Exactly what I say. You have an opportunity—now—to prove that my words don't apply to you. Make an effort to get to the heart of things. The men in this factory spend their lives in a struggle for bare existence. Can you expect them to be contented, to shut their eyes to

34

the high possibilities of life, and not stretch out their hands to grasp the passing prizes of toil ? Instead of an earnest and sympathetic wish to understand their just aspirations, and a real desire to find a lasting settlement, you meet them with suspicion and platitudes ; and their employer meets them with resentment and threats.

MEN : Yes—yes ! that's it !

RODERICK WENALLT : Wait ! You misrepresent my attitude entirely. Your indictment is an appeal to ignorance and passion.

JENKIN LEWIS : They have had a rise many times. You don't say anything about that, Llewelyn Garth.

RODERICK WENALLT (*with a laugh*) : It wouldn't do for an agitator to tell the truth : it would spoil his game.

LADY VIOLET : Games are generally played by sportsmen. I am sorry you are so unfair, Roderick. I haven't heard Mr. Garth say anything to justify what you say.

LLEWELYN GARTH : Thank you, Lady Violet. I don't wish to conceal the truth. It is true, the men have had a rise in wages from time to time, but it hasn't kept pace with the rise in the standard of living. Education is bearing its natural fruit, and those who forced it upon the people must accept its consequences. I appeal to you, Mr. Lewis. Try to realise how you would feel if you were forced to live as they do in their miserable cottages.

LADY VIOLET : Indeed, many of them are not fit to live in.

WILKIN WATKINS : It is always April with them—enough rain coming through the thatch to turn the factory wheel. Do very well for people fond of water, like the Baptists, but not for respectable Church of England people. You can fish in them when there is a flood, and be sure to catch the Ague or something nasty. You can't be joyful in them, Mr. Lewis.

JENKIN LEWIS : What is that fool talking about ?

WILKIN WATKINS : I was thinking about the old pike in the factory pond living on the little fishes, and not knowing the difference between a spoon-bait and a real minnow. It's easy enough to catch him (*chuckles*).

The MEN *laugh.*

JENKIN LEWIS : You laugh, do you ?

LADY VIOLET : You must laugh or cry sometimes, Mr. Lewis, and Wilkin helps us to laugh. It's a pity we can't look at other people's troubles as we look at our own : it would insure their consideration from a human point of view.

LLEWELYN GARTH : And help politicians to forget that they are out for plunder. I ask you, Mr.

Lewis, I ask you, Matthew, to remember that your interests are the same. One can do nothing without the other. The ruin of the masters would mean the ruin of the men. If you would only realise that simple truth, and act upon it in a spirit of mutual trust, you would do more to put an end to trade disputes than Party has ever done.

MEN : That's the truth. We are all with you there, Mr. Garth.

RODERICK WENALLT *shakes his head, and paces the room smiling cynically.*

LADY VIOLET : Mr. Garth puts things in an intensely interesting light. Don't you think he is right, Roderick ?

RODERICK WENALLT : My dear Violet, I'll think anything humanly possible to oblige you. But where Parliament has failed, the individual is not likely to succeed. Novices are really very bold creatures, quite ready to step in where Statesmen fear to tread. The old adage is still applicable.

LLEWELYN GARTH : You waste your sarcasm upon me, Mr. Wenallt. But for individual effort, there would be no collective effort. Party Government is a curse ; and so long as Party men reap their richest harvest on the field of strife, they will keep the ring for the combatants, with their tongue in their cheek. There is not a man in your Party free to obey his conscience.

RODERICK WENALLT : Indeed ?   What does he obey then ?

LLEWELYN GARTH :   The crack of the Party Whip.

JACOB MORGAN :   Just so.   He must grovel or die.

JENKIN LEWIS :   Don't meddle with things you don't understand, Jacob Morgan.   You are not an M.P. yet—if you are a J.P.

WILKIN WATKINS :   M.P. would suit me grand. Give me £400 a year, and I will treat everybody to everything.

LADY VIOLET :   Bravo ! Wilkin.   You know how to promise, and that is the chief qualification of a Candidate (*laughing.*)   Oh, Mr. Garth, why don't you put Wilkin up to stand against my cousin ? It would be splendid !

RODERICK WENALLT (*with a grim laugh*) : 'Pon my word, Violet, I didn't expect to hear such nonsense from you.

LLEWELYN GARTH :   It's the kind of wise nonsense, Lady Violet, that would bring home to the electors the absurdity of the Party System.   Tie the Party ticket around the devil's neck, and he would be elected against an angel.   What do you say, Wilkin ?   Will you fight Mr. Wenallt at the next election ?

WILKIN WATKINS :   Indeed, I don't know—

THE GREAT EXPERIMENT

perhaps there is too much of the angel in me to
fight against him, and win.

LADY VIOLET : You are no sportsman, Wilkin,
or you'd take your chance of a fall in a scramble for
£400 a year.

WILKIN WATKINS (*chuckles*) : Oh, if there's
sport, I'm on. I will fight the best man (*poses and
dodges in a pugilistic attitude*) in the village for
£400 a year, and be joyful over it ; but I don't say
I'll beat him. You can buy a lot of plaster with that
to patch you after the battle—if you are not down
amongst the dead men. Let us be joyful, whatever.

LADY VIOLET : What fun ! Roderick, you'll
have to look to yourself.

LLEWELYN GARTH (*paces the room thoughtfully*):
If I had power—if I had wealth ! (*A pause.*)

LADY VIOLET : If you had, what would you do
with them ?

RODERICK WENALLT (*cynically*) : He would
be a tinker to mend the broken pots of the universe,
and make another world out of them of a brand new
pattern.

LADY VIOLET : Don't be cynical, Roderick.
What would you do with wealth and power, if you
had them, Mr. Garth ?

LLEWELYN GARTH : I would devote all I pos-
sessed to the destruction of Party Government.
Parliament should be freed from its thraldom, and

39

become once more mistress of the destinies of the people and not the bond-slave of Ministers. Mercenaries should make way for free men, and the individual conscience should decide the fate of human problems.

RODERICK WENALLT : Are there no other little things you would like to do ?

LLEWELYN GARTH : Oh, yes !—I would set up a Factory of my own, and run it on new lines.

JENKIN LEWIS (*furiously*) : What did I tell you ? There is the truth at last. He 'ould set up a Factory against me ; and he calls himself my friend.

RODERICK WENALLT : Of course ! He would call it healthy competition. The individual conscience stretches wonderfully under the strain of self-interest.

LLEWELYN GARTH : Self-interest ? Yes ! You speak truer than you think. I would make it the self-interest of every man to run an even handicap for the great prizes of life, and put out all his strength to win. I would give the men a share in the profits, and induce them to take a personal interest in our common fortunes.

MATTHEW *and the* WORKMEN *listen eagerly, break into a cheer, put their heads together, and talk in excited whispers.*

RODERICK WENALLT : They might do that if they were part owners.

LLEWELYN GARTH : That is what I should make them. I should pay them by results. What they made above their living wage they should have in shares. In this way, the principle of Co-opera-tion——

RODERICK WENALLT (*interrupts with a laugh*): Lord Robert Cecil's prize packet appropriated by the Political Tinker ! What do you think of it, Mr. Lewis ?

JENKIN LEWIS : I don't think nothing of it— nothing ! It is confiscation—corruption—robbery !

MATTHEW JONES : Don't say that, Mr. Lewis. Indeed it is a big chance for all of us. In the name of God ! take it, and you will never be sorry that you listened to Llewelyn Garth, and trusted us. We are men as independent as you are, and don't like to feel that we are servants. We want work, and we can work, and will make your Factory the pride of the place and a pattern for others to follow. Manage it in your own way ; sell what we make at your own price. What will satisfy you will satisfy us, and make everybody prosperous and contented.

JENKIN LEWIS *paces the room restlessly.* ARLAIS *comes in, joins* GARTH, *whispers to him.* GARTH *shakes his head.* ARLAIS *watches her father anxiously.*).

LADY VIOLET (*coaxingly*) : It is a golden opportunity, Mr. Lewis.

41

JENKIN LEWIS : Yes, indeed, a golden opportunity to spend money on others.

JACOB MORGAN (*earnestly*) : It is a great chance. It is the right way, friend Jenkin—the only way.

MATTHEW JONES (*earnestly*) : For the sake of peace, Mr. Lewis—for the sake of peace !

LLEWELYN GARTH : The welfare of all these men and their families—and more than that : more than you dream of—is in your hands, Mr. Lewis. It is the parting of the ways. A false step now will be as disastrous to you as to them.

JENKIN LEWIS : Oh, you threaten me, do you ?

LADY VIOLET (*interposes hastily*) : No one threatens you. But I see, you are upset. Think it over until to-morrow, and give your answer then.

JENKIN LEWIS : No, I will give my answer now. I will not do it. The Factory is mine, and I will keep it.

LLEWELYN GARTH : I am sorry—very sorry. What are you going to do, Matthew ?

MATTHEW JONES (*to his fellow workmen*) : Boys ?

THE MEN (*sombrely—passionately*) : Strike ! strike !

MATTHEW JONES : This time there will be no giving in.

ONE MAN : No ! not this time !

42

ANOTHER MAN : No—not this time, by God !

JENKIN LEWIS : You have said that before, but you have had to give in.

LLEWELYN GARTH (*with emotion*) : Is that your last word, Mr. Lewis ?

ARLAIS LEWIS : Oh, father ! remember what a strike means for all of us.

JENKIN LEWIS (*bitterly*) : Are you, my own daughter, turning against me ?

ARLAIS LEWIS : No. But the thought of a strike and the misery it will bring make me afraid. I have longed to be home with you, and now, instead of peace and happiness, there is to be strife, anger and ruin ! Oh, do not let a chance of peace slip by, for my sake !

JENKIN LEWIS (*regards* ARLAIS *with troubled eyes—feeling her appeal deeply*) : You don't understand these things, my girl. I would do anything in the world for you that was reasonable ; but I can't play into the hands of my enemies. It is principle with me.

LLEWELYN GARTH (*in low, passionate voice, to* JENKIN LEWIS) : We are not your enemies ! You don't know your enemies from your friends. God help you ! You'll find out the truth some day— when it is too late.

ARLAIS *walks slowly from her father, with bowed head, almost sobbing.* GARTH *follows her, and tries*

43

*to console her, passing with her into the parlour, R.
There is a tense silence.*

MATTHEW JONES : Come, boys ! (*The* MEN
*troop out, B—some sullenly, some gloomily anxious.
At the door,* MATTHEW *turns, looks steadily, reproachfully, at* JENKIN LEWIS, *and then follows the
others out. There is a pause.*)

LADY VIOLET (*sadly*) : This is a bad beginning,
Mr. Lewis. Where will it end ?

JENKIN LEWIS : Don't blame me. It is Garth's
fault.

RODERICK WENALLT : Who is this man, that
he should presume to take your affairs into his
hands ? Who is he ? Who is he ?

JENKIN LEWIS : He is the adopted son of Jacob
Morgan.

RODERICK WENALLT : That means anything
or nothing. What is he ? Perhaps Mr. Morgan
will enlighten us ?

JACOB MORGAN : Garth's good name is in his
own keeping, and it will be time enough for you to
ask questions about him when he dishonours it.

LADY VIOLET *sympathetically grasps* JACOB
MORGAN'S *hand, and tries to soothe his wounded
feelings.* GARTH *comes in slowly, from the parlour,
R.* LADY VIOLET *meets him.* RODERICK WEN-
ALLT *is about to say something. She stops him with
a gesture.*

44

LADY VIOLET : Mr. Garth—I want you to come and see Lord Wenallt. He may be able to suggest some means to bring this unfortunate dispute to an end. Will you come ? (GARTH *looks at her earnestly—hesitates—seems on the point of speaking.*)

RODERICK WENALLT : It wouldn't be any use. Remember, Lord Wenallt is the leader of a great Party, and wouldn't care to discuss trade disputes under these circumstances.

JACOB MORGAN : Come, Garth. (*Takes* GARTH'S *arm, and leads him B.*).

LADY VIOLET (*ignoring* RODERICK WENALLT) : You will come, Mr. Garth ? (GARTH *pauses.*) I ask you to come as a favour to me—for the sake of the villagers.

LLEWELYN GARTH (*hesitates*) : If I thought I could do any good——

RODERICK WENALLT (*interrupts*) : Ah ! I see, I shall have to talk to his lordship, and prepare him for the honour of discussing high politics with an adopted son from heaven knows where.

LADY VIOLET : Roderick !

RODERICK WENALLT : No—it will never do. Why, you can't enter a horse for a race without giving his pedigree.

JACOB MORGAN (*with a furious glance at* RODERICK WENALLT) : Come, Garth—let us go home. (*Goes out indignantly, B.*).

45

LLEWELYN GARTH (*slowly, thoughtfully, follows* JACOB MORGAN ; *turns at the door, looks straight at* LADY VIOLET, *who is looking very distressed*) : I will come, Lady Violet. (*Exit.*)

CURTAIN.

ACT II.

A Week Later.

—

SCENE I.—*Outside White Barn in front of a plantation. There is a clear space in the foreground, fringed with bushes, mountain ash, saplings, and clumps of gorse and broom. As the curtain rises, JENKIN LEWIS' WORKMEN are seen gathering in front of the barn, and a hum of conversation is heard. MATTHEW JONES climbs into a wheelbarrow.*

—

MATTHEW JONES : Boys ! you know what we are meeting for ?

(Cries of " Yes—Yes.")

TOM SAIS *(a gruff workman, in truculent voice)* : To settle old Jenkin Lewis, and have done with him once and for all.

MATTHEW JONES : No ! Tom Sais : to settle our dispute with him.

TOM SAIS : Same thing. If it wasn't for him there'd be no dispute. He's been trampling on us long enough,—and we've got to trample on him or lie in the mud for him to walk over us when he likes.

ONE OF THE MEN : You're right, Tom.

RODERICK WENALLT *observes the scene from behind some bushes by the side of the Barn. He keeps out of sight of the men, who are unaware of his presence.*

47

MATTHEW JONES : Now, look here, boys, Tom Sais has only been working at the Factory about nine days, and it's no good him talking as if he was grey with trouble in the Factory. If he was a bit more modest, he 'ouldn't talk so loud. The thing is, What are we going to do—go on fighting or give in !

(Cries from the MEN) : Fight—fight to the end ?

TOM SAIS : Burn down the Factory about the old devil's ears. That's the only way to bring a man like him to his senses.

Some of the MEN *applaud ; others look doubtfully at* MATTHEW, *and murmur uneasily.*

MATTHEW JONES (*climbs down out of the barrow*): I am not going to listen to talk like that. We don't burn down factories in Carmarthenshire, Tom Sais, because of a dispute about wages. No ! we are not that sort, thank God ! What 'ould you say if Jenkin Lewis pulled down your cottage and drove you out to starve on the road 'till you gave in ? Answer me that !

TOM SAIS : That's all my eye. It's not the same thing by long chalks. Why, the cottage belongs to him, and he's not such a fool as to pull down his own property.

MATTHEW JONES : And if the Factory was yours 'ould you set fire to it ? No ! But you are not talking straight and honest. We are going to fight with clean hands. That's Mr. Garth's motto, eh, boys ? And we are going to stick to it, and not bring disgrace on the place.

SOME OF THE MEN : Aie—Aie ! Matthew, so we will.

TOM SAIS (*jumps into the barrow*) : Clean hands means no work and starvation, and you'll have plenty of that if you listen to such slush. Who's Mr. Garth, I should like to know ? He's no workman. A sort of half-and-half, that's what I'd call him. What's he done for us ? I ask you ! (*looks round sneeringly*). Echo answers not a blooming ha'-p'orth ! Talks about his stock-in-trade. Bah ! I hates a mealy-mouthed chap what's saying his prayers when he ought to be doin' business. Are we a lot of sheep to be driven by the first mongrel that comes yapping at our heels ?

The MEN *shout* : " Not likely. Go ahead, Tom !"

MATTHEW : Hold hard, boys ! If you are going against Garth, to follow Tom Sais, you had better know where he is going to lead you before it is too late.

TOM SAIS : Bah ! You're Garth's man. Go and bring him here. I'll talk to him ! (*Some of the* MEN *laugh and cheer.*)

MATTHEW JONES (*distressed*) : I am sorry things have gone like this, boys, and you will be sorry, too, if you follow a wild man like—(*points to* TOM SAIS)—him.

49

TOM SAIS (*with a provoking laugh*) : **Poor old Matthew !** He knows I'm a better man for this job than he is, and he's jealous. (*The* MEN *laugh.*)

MATTHEW *turns away from them slowly, sorrowfully.*

MATTHEW JONES (*half-turning, and speaking earnestly*) : I am going to fetch Mr. Garth ; and I beg of you, for your own sakes, not to do anything until he comes.

MATTHEW *hurries away.*

TOM SAIS : A couple of pints of beer, with a dash of brandy in it, that's what Matthew wants. He's got no heart (*laughs jeeringly*). Gather round, boys, and listen to what I've got to say to you. We're all of one mind, ain't we ? (MEN *shout* "Aie, Aie.") Then we've got to win this fight. (*The* MEN *shout* "Yes, Yes."). Right ! All you've got to do is to keep your mouths shut, and leave the bizniss to me. Is that a bargain ?

The MEN *consult together eagerly.*

TOM SAIS : If you trust me, hold up your hands, and it's as good as done. I'll win the fight, and you can have the credit.

The MEN *hold up their hands, and cheer, and cry,* "We are with you, TOM."

TOM SAIS : Ah ! now you're men ! You'll be glad to-morrow that you haven't behaved like sheep. (*Looks at watch*) Three o'clock. It's a bit early yet. We'll let old Jenkin go home to his tea, and then we'll make an afternoon call at the Factory, and leave our cards. How's that for a joke? (*The* MEN *laugh and cry, "Good old* TOM.") Pity we haven't got some nets. We might take him a few rabbits, or leave 'em at home by mistake (*searches his coat pockets.*). By gum! forgot all about 'em (*takes a bag with a ferret in it from one pocket, and some nets from another, and hands them to one of the men*). There you are, lads—what you may call a merciful dispensation—ain't it? Go ahead, and I'll stay here and watch for the Keepers. If you hear me shout, run like the devil.

The MEN *hurry off into the plantation.* TOM SAIS *waits until they are out of hearing, and then gives a low whistle.* RODERICK WENALLT *comes from behind the Barn and joins him.*

TOM SAIS (*with a grin of satisfaction*): It's come off all right, sir. You'll have Garth in the net before you're an hour older.

RODERICK WENALLT: You've earned your money, Tom, and I expect you'll want it, if you carry out your programme. It's pretty hot.

TOM SAIS: Hah! about as hot as fire.

RODERICK WENALLT: 'Sh! Be careful, man (*looks round him nervously*). My Keepers are behind the barn. If they overheard you, it would go hard with you.

51

TOM SAIS (*loudly—with a grin*): And what about you? (RODERICK WENALLT *starts with alarm.*) Them bein' there makes the risk more and the price higher. Lucky you brought 'em, sir. There's no limited liability about our bit of bizniss. Oh, no! it's a equal risk for both—big profits and quick returns, or—limbo.

RODERICK WENALLT: Be quiet! Don't talk like a fool (*thrusts bank notes into* TOM'S *hands*).

TOM SAIS (*reckoning notes*): £50 I makes it. When you calls a man a fool, sir, especially one as has happened to help you in a delicate bit of bizniss, you've got to pay extra to soothe his ruffled feelins, especially when there's witnesses in the shape of two honest keepers to testify to the langwidge. And there's the matter of the fire. There's a bit more to pay on that—by way of insurance (*laughs facetiously—holds out his hand*).

RODERICK WENALLT *looks at him.* TOM'S *grin broadens, and then his jaw sets in a stern expression, almost threatening. Reluctantly,* RODERICK WENALLT *hands him some more notes—doling them out one by one—*TOM *nodding as each reaches his hand,* RODERICK WENALLT *stops.*

RODERICK WENALLT (*shakes his head*): No more!

TOM SAIS: Keep on doin' it, Mr. Wenallt. It's a fine exercise for a generous heart.

RODERICK WENALLT : Not another shilling.

TOM SAIS : Quite right, sir ; I only takes paper (*holds out his hand*). A final fiver, by way of thanks offerin', and' we'll wind up the bizness—O.K.

RODERICK WENALLT (*thrusts another note into* TOM'S *hand*) : You've taken advantage of me. But I'll remember it.

TOM SAIS : Law, sir ! rememberin' things is my strong point. It *was* my intention to forget this little bizniss, but there ! if you remember it I can't do no less.

RODERICK WENALLT (*tries to laugh it off*) : You're a humorist, Tom. (*Suddenly holds up his hand for silence—listens.*) Some one's running this way.

TOM SAIS : Garth, I expect.

RODERICK WENALLT (*nods—hurriedly in low voice*) : You'll clear out to-night ? (*moving towards barn*).

TOM SAIS : Yes. It'll be too hot to hold me after this.

RODERICK WENALLT (*pointing*) : That's your way. Run !

TOM SAIS *runs off.* RODERICK WENALLT *gives a low signal, and in a few moments two* KEEPERS *appear from behind the barn.*

RODERICK WENALLT (*points to gorse bushes behind the wheelbarrow*) : Get behind the gorse.

53

(KEEPERS *crouch behind the gorse.*) **You know what to do ?** (*One of the* KEEPERS *shows his head and nods.*) **Remember, he's the leader of this gang of poachers, and you've got to get him** (*he listens with his hand to his ear*). **He's coming !** (*Conceals himself behind the barn.*)

The next moment GARTH *runs up with a swinging stride, and stops suddenly when he finds the place deserted.*

LLEWELYN GARTH (*panting from exertion*): **The fools !** (*Sits on the wheelbarrow to rest.*) **Am I too late ?**

The two KEEPERS *spring suddenly upon* GARTH, *who is too surprised to struggle.* RODERICK WEN-ALLT *saunters up.*)

RODERICK WENALLT : Good day, Mr. Garth. Poaching is a risky amusement for a man of character. I fancy you are caught out this time.

DROP CURTAIN.

ACT II.

The Same Evening.

—

SCENE II.—*The Library, Wenallt Castle. Balcony showing through open French windows, richly curtained at back. Trees and grounds beyond. Door R.*

—

As the curtain rises LADY WENALLT *and* LADY VIOLET *are seen coming in, R, talking animatedly, the former leaning on* LADY VIOLET'S *arm.*

LADY WENALLT : How can you talk so foolishly ! (*sits down*).

LADY VIOLET : Is it foolish to be natural—to speak as you feel and think ? Indeed, Mr. Garth is the kind of man any girl would run risks for. But do not fear ! Am I not engaged to my chivalrous cousin ?—used as a bit of cement to keep two estates together ?

LADY VIOLET : Violet dear ! I wish you wouldn't talk so wildly.

LADY VIOLET (*a little bitterly*) : Wildly ? Oh, no ! I'm merely discussing an excellent business arrangement. What more could a girl desire than to be married to a sophisticated man of the world, who would know how to keep her in order, and permit her to spend her own money—or as much of it as he didn't devote to his own pleasures ? Poor

speak from your heart—just as - - as Mr. Garth does—if you could forget that horrid Parliament, and be your real self.

LORD WENALLT : You don't know how I've longed to do so. But you mustn't beguile me into such realms of fancy. What did Jacob Morgan say about it all ?

LADY VIOLET : He didn't say much ; but he was very, very angry with Roderick. There is a sleeping lion in that old man, and Roderick roused it.

LORD WENALLT : Ah ! then he is fond of Garth ?

LADY VIOLET : Proud of him, too, I think.

LORD WENALLT : I'm glad to hear that. Jacob Morgan is a man of sterling character—a gentleman at heart. Remember that, Violet, if ever you cross his path.

LADY VIOLET : I love the dear old man, and I think he loves me.

LORD WENALLT : Everyone loves you, child. How did the young man—Garth—bear himself under Roderick's provocation ?

LADY VIOLET : At first he seemed surprised ; but he soon raised his head and looked Roderick straight in the face. As I watched him, there came into his face now and then an expression that I have only seen in the Wenallts when they have been deeply moved (*looks intently at* LORD WENALLT). You have it now. That is very strange.

LORD WENALLT : Oh, I don't know. The Wenallts have no patent for their features.

LADY WENALLT : He bore himself like—(*hesitates*)—like a Wenallt, did he, child ?

LADY VIOLET : Yes. But I'm sure he felt Roderick's unfriendliness very much. I was sorry for him.

LORD WENALLT (*to himself*) : He showed the blood of a fighting race. The harder some men are hit, the higher they rise.

LADY VIOLET (*coldly—to* LADY WENALLT) : I didn't know you were so interested in Mr. Garth. You were not just now.

LADY WENALLT : I am interested in all brave men who fight their battles alone, and ask for nothing better than a fair field for the struggle. It seems to me that (*looks fixed at* LORD WENALLT) one of the greatest privileges in life is to hold out a helping hand to such men.

LORD WENALLT : What ! and rob them of half the credit of success ? It's bad farming to cut your corn before it's ripe. We both mean the same thing, Margaret, only you want to anticipate things a little —eh ? The woman in you cries out against cold calculation ; and the man in me whispers, " Not just yet."

59

LORD WENALLT : You'll vote from your heart, and not from your head, eh, Wilkin ?

WILKIN WATKINS (*nods vigorously*) : I suppose I can go now, my lord ?

LORD WENALLT : Yes, you rascal—go.

WILKIN WATKINS (*looking at a big hole in his coat, and pushing his hand through it*) : I suppose your lordship hasn't got an old coat to give me ? I am very shabby to come to a grand house like this.

LORD WENALLT : I dare say I have.

WILKIN WATKINS (*chuckles*) : A red one I 'ould like—to run after the hounds, and cut the fox's tail off for Lady Violet. It 'ould look lovely in her hat.   And if I had some top-boots, I 'ould wear them both together, and be a real sportsman like your lordship.

LORD WENALLT (*laughing*) : Wilkin, you must come and see me again (*walks across the room thoughtfully*).   Take him to Williams, Violet, and let him have what he wants.

LADY VIOLET (*gaily*) : Come along, Wilkin.

WILKIN WATKINS : Thank you, my lord.   I will remember you when I go fishing next time— whether I am an M.P. or no (*chuckles*).

Exunt LADY VIOLET *and* WILKIN.   LADY WEN-ALLT *follows them out slowly, thoughtfully, watched by* LORD WENALLT.

LORD WENALLT (*paces the room slowly,—to*

THE GREAT EXPERIMENT

himself) : It's been a hard test for the boy—a tremendous test ! (*The* FOOTMAN *opens the door a little—retires softly—leaving the impression that he is listening.*) But if I had a dozen sons, I would send them out into the world's rough nursery, as I sent Garth.

LADY VIOLET *comes in laughing.*

LADY VIOLET : Just **look** ! Isn't he gorgeous ?

WILKIN *is seen in the doorway struggling into a pink coat. He trots into the room, with a chuckle, followed by the* FOOTMAN, *carrying a pair of top-boots.*

FOOTMAN (*solemnly*) : Does your lordship wish me to put the boots on the—the gentleman or on the chair ?

WILKIN WATKINS : Here—give them to me. Chairs don't wear boots, you silly fellow (*seizes top-boots, kicks off his old shoes, sits down on the carpet, and tries to pull on the top-boots, but fails.*) Gosh ! here's a job ! It is the old trouses that is doing it. They are not used to top-boots. Perhaps your lordship has got a pair of breeches that *is* used to them ? (*gets up*).

LORD WENALLT (*laughing*) : Take him with you, Williams, and give him a pair.

FOOTMAN : Yes, my lord. Kindly follow me, Mr. Watkins.

63

FOOTMAN *goes out, followed by* WILKIN, *who imitates his dignified deportment.*

LADY VIOLET : How very human you are—for a Cabinet Minister (*winds her arms round his neck, and rests her cheek against his shoulder.*)

LORD WENALLT : You and Wilkin would make a crocodile human.

LADY VIOLET : Oh ! (*smiles up at* LORD WENALLT). I think Mr. Garth is coming to see you to-day (*runs out*).

LORD WENALLT *directs some envelopes, pauses, listens, glances towards the window expectantly, stamps the envelopes, rings bell, crosses to balcony.*)

FOOTMAN *enters.*

LORD WENALLT (*handing letters to* FOOTMAN) : See that these letters are posted.

FOOTMAN : Yes, my lord.

LORD WENALLT : And, Williams—If Mr. Garth should call, I will see him.

FOOTMAN : Yes, my lord. (*Exit.*)

LORD WENALLT *steps out on to the balcony, and is seen walking to-and-fro outside.* RODERICK WENALLT *enters quickly,* R, *followed by* GARTH, *in charge of two* GAMEKEEPERS. LORD WENALLT *looks in from the balcony with a stare of surprise.*

LORD WENALLT : Hello ! Roderick—what's the meaning of this ? (*coming in, his eyes fixed on* GARTH).

RODERICK WENALLT (*to one of the* KEEPERS) :
You'd better explain to his lordship, Rogers.

KEEPER : Caught him and a lot of strikers
poaching, my lord, in the barn plantation.

GARTH *is disdainfully silent.*

LORD WENALLT (*incredulously*) : Poaching ?
Surely, you have made a mistake ?

KEEPER : No, my lord, we caught him red-
handed.

LORD WENALLT (*vexed*) : I am sorry to hear
this. What have you to say, Mr. Garth ?

LLEWELYN GARTH : It is untrue. It is a
trumped-up story to discredit me.

RODERICK WENALLT : Of course—you'd say
that. Don't you think it would pay you better to
own up ? The leader of a mob of strikers has to do
a good many lawless things before he's properly
appreciated, you know. That's the sort of certi-
ficate or character that gives a man like you power.
(*Signs to the* KEEPER) Go on, Rogers.

KEEPER : We found him near the White Barn
watching, while the others were netting rabbits in
the wood, my lord.

LORD WENALLT : Was he alone ?

The KEEPER *hestitates, and looks to* RODERICK
WENALLT *to answer.*

RODERICK WENALLT : There were others ;
but Rogers has told you that they were in the wood.

LORD WENALLT : You saw them, I suppose ?

RODERICK WENALLT : We heard them and saw them.

LORD WENALLT : Why did you let the others go ?

RODERICK WENALLT : Oh, they're small fry. I wanted to make sure of this man—their acknowledged leader.

LLEWELYN GARTH (*quietly*) : A leader, Lord Wenallt, is one who leads. Unfortunately, the men broke away from me. As a Parliamentary leader, you must know what it is to be thrown over by reckless or nervous followers. Gratitude is not the strong point of those whom you try to serve.

LORD WENALLT : You are young to have that experience.

LLEWELYN GARTH (*shrugs his shoulders*) : The charge of poaching is a malicious invention, so far as I am concerned. I have many farmer friends and leave to shoot on their lands when I want to. As for the others, they have been tricked and misled by a man who is no friend of mine : a violent, uneducated fellow named Tom Sais, who obtained employment at the factory (*looks straight at* RODERICK WENALLT) on Mr. Wenallt's recommendation.

RODERICK WENALLT : Do you suggest that I am responsible for Tom Sais' conduct ?

LLEWELYN GARTH : I don't think I should be

66

wrong if I did. Your name is always on his lips. He boasts of your friendship, holds you up as a man after his own heart, and scoffs when my name is mentioned. He is a man, my lord, who hasn't got the brains to act without prompting ; and I say he is Mr. Wenallt's creature, and that he's been put up to drag the men into mischief and make me responsible for them.

RODERICK WENALLT : And I say you have used the opportunity of the dispute between Jenkin Lewis and his workmen to play Providence to the men and Devil to the master—to preach the gospel of "Everything for nothing." An excellent text, I admit, when you've got nothing. But poor old Jenkin Lewis owns the factory ; so he must be made to pay—to share his income with you and your friends. To a man who preaches robbery of that sort, poaching must be a pleasant pastime.

LLEWELYN GARTH : Your hostility is leading you into dangerous depths, Mr. Wenallt—at least, there would be danger if anyone took you seriously. If it gives you any pleasure to draw fancy situations, you are likely to enjoy full scope for the exercise of your unenviable art, so far as I am concerned. (*turns his back upon* RODERICK WENALLT).

RODERICK WENALLT : You are clever, sir. You know how to slide over thin ice ; but I notice you don't contradict me ?

LLEWELYN GARTH (*to* LORD WENALLT) : *I* do not, but the facts do.

LORD WENALLT : Ah ! the facts are all important. I have had an opportunity of learning something about Mr. Garth. Lady Violet has given me a full account of what happened at the factory the other day (RODERICK WENALLT *bites his lips*). I gathered the impression that he was rather a restraining influence upon the men. (*To* GARTH) : Will you tell me how you came to be in the wood ?

LLEWELYN GARTH : Willingly, my lord. There was a meeting of the men at the White Barn, arranged by Tom Sais. I was told nothing about it.

RODERICK WENALLT : Then how came you to be there ?

LLEWELYN GARTH : I was hurriedly fetched by Matthew Jones. He, my lord, is a straightforward, level-headed man, and was much upset by what had taken place at the meeting. He told me that Tom Sais had spoken very wildly, and suggested setting fire to the factory.

LORD WENALLT : This is serious—very serious ! Anarchists in Carmarthenshire ! Did you hear anything of this dangerous talk, Roderick ?

RODERICK WENALLT : I heard that and a great deal more ; and I was so alarmed that I determined to bring the leader of these rash men to account.

LORD WENALLT (*thoughtfully*) : I see. I don't blame you. But it might have been better to get hold of Tom Sais. He seems to be the fire-brand of the party.

RODERICK WENALLT : I'm sorry now I didn't. In the excitement of the moment I overlooked the fellow's importance.

LORD WENALLT : Go on with your story, Mr. Garth.

LLEWELYN GARTH : I rushed off to the meeting. The men had gone. These two Keepers sprang upon me suddenly, and dragged me off here. That is all I know about it. I meant to see you to-day, my lord, but not quite in this fashion.

LORD WENALLT (*to the* KEEPERS) : Have you anything to say ?

KEEPERS : No, my lord. We only did what we were ordered.

LORD WENALLT : Then you can go.

The KEEPERS *salute, and go out.*

LORD WENALLT : It seems to me that you've been made the victim of other men's faults, Mr. Garth.

RODERICK WENALLT : If he has, he can easily set himself right. Let him throw over these strikers, condemn their lawless conduct, and disown his Socialism.

LLEWELYN GARTH : A man who is not a

69

Socialist can't disown Socialism. Perhaps, I am too small a man, Lord Wenallt, for you to trouble what I am ; but I will venture in self-defence to claim my right to think for myself and to fight for my liberty of action. I am what I am—a labourer in the every-day world, striving to make the lot of the toilers better ; and Mr. Wenallt can't make me a traitor to my instincts by trumping up charges against me and putting a false label on my back.

LORD WENALLT (*after an interval of deep consideration*): Excuse me a moment, Mr. Garth. (*Takes* RODERICK WENALLT *aside—speaks to him earnestly.*).

LADY VIOLET *looks in from the French window, smiles at* GARTH, *who bows gravely to her. In a few moments* RODERICK WENALLT *approaches* GARTH, *with a forced smile.* LORD WENALLT *watches him, and then crosses to* LADY VIOLET. GARTH'S *eyes are fixed upon, and his attention is absorbed by, a picture of a child on the wall.*

RODERICK WENALLT : Lord Wenallt has convinced me that I owe you an apology, Mr. Garth. I need not tell you that I am always ready to accept his judgment in a matter of this sort, and act upon it. I am sorry. (GARTH *bows.*)

LORD WENALLT : Handsomely said, Roderick.

RODERICK WENALLT : I hope we shall be good friends in future, Mr. Garth.

70

LLEWELYN GARTH : That will depend upon you.

LADY VIOLET (*coming in*) : I shall begin to like you, Roderick, if you behave so nicely.

RODERICK WENALLT (*puts his hand to his heart, and bows*) : Now that we have signed a treaty of peace, Mr. Garth, and you have declared for law and order, I hope that you and I may become allies, and fight this election on the same side.

LLEWELYN GARTH : I am not a Party man, Mr. Wenallt, and can't fight for either side.

RODERICK WENALLT : Put in a word for me, Violet. I want Mr. Garth's help badly ; and you are all-powerful, you know.

LADY VIOLET : I have no influence with Mr. Garth.

RODERICK WENALLT : My dear girl, your eyes are lodestones to attract all unfixed human elements and lead men away to any romantic or political spot you choose.

LADY VIOLET : You hear, Mr. Garth ? Won't you come with us to The Promised Land ?

LLEWELYN GARTH (*smiling*) : I'm afraid we shouldn't travel very far together. There are no politics in The Promised Land, and that wouldn't suit Mr. Wenallt.

RODERICK WENALLT : My dear fellow, don't wander away from rational landmarks. The Pro-

mised Land is a child's dream—a nursery rhyme—
a myth. No, thank you, I don't go in for experi-
mental politics or freak problems.

LLEWELYN GARTH (*good-naturedly*) : No—you
are a disciple of the cut-and-dried school—a passen-
ger in the lumbering old coach that always jolts
along in the same old ruts.

LADY VIOLET : You have no imagination,
Roderick, or you would understand that the chief
charm of Mr. Garth's Eden is the absence of politicians. What do you say, Guardian ?

LORD WENALLT (*laughing*) : I think you are
right, child. It would be a veritable haven of rest
for disenchanted Party politicians.

LLEWELYN GARTH : We may get there, my
lord, if we will it. But it would be over the body of
the Party Bogey.

LORD WENALLT : I don't think I should regret
that. I have had a surfeit of Party. There isn't a
word in the dictionary that I have got to dislike so
much. Party—Party—Party ! It's dinned into my
ears as though it were some sacred symbol to judge
everything by. It fences round personal freedom,
limits the liberty of conscience, and blurs the true
perspective of things. No—I should not regret it.

RODERICK WENALLT : You take my breath
away ! Surely, you are not going to throw up
office, let the reins of power drop from your hands,

72

and join a rotten old procession of caravans—to goodness knows where ? My dear uncle, in severe earnest—Are you going to desert us ?

LADY VIOLET (*looking out of the window*) : *I* am. I'm going to meet Wilkin. He's strutting up the drive, smoking a cigar (*runs out*).

LLEWELYN GARTH : To follow one's conscience is not desertion, Mr. Wenallt.

RODERICK WENALLT : Call it what you like —to desert your Party is treachery.

LORD WENALLT : To desert your Country for the sake of your Party—What is that, Roderick ? You ought to think before you speak. (*Picks up a newspaper, and points to a paragraph*) Read that, Mr. Garth.

LLEWELYN GARTH (*takes the paper and reads*) : " American journals sharply criticise Washington because, in a case where dollars were concerned, the Executive took prompt action, but in a case where the usages of mere civilisation are at stake there seems a lack of administrative initiative, which is ascribed to the paralysing influence of Party politics." (GARTH *pauses—looks up.*)

LORD WENALLT : That's a pleasant reflection, isn't it ? Go on.

LLEWELYN GARTH (*reads*) : " Baby-killing by German bomb-throwers is a mere question of sentiment, urge blind partisans here, and to send a protest

73

to Germany would alienate the support of many voters "—(*breaks off*). It's brutal !

LORD WENALLT : Could the shame and failure of Party Government be more nakedly exposed ? On the one side innocent lives ; on the other Party interests ; and Party interests let the lives be sacrificed. It has burned itself deeply into my brain.

LLEWELYN GARTH : Here's another paragraph, my lord, I should like to read. (*Reads*) : " In war the normal working of the Party system can not be operative without the risk of profound injury, and even destruction to a Nation."

LORD WENALLT : They were the words of one of my colleagues.

RODERICK WENALLT : But your colleague only spoke of the Party system in time of war.

LORD WENALLT : And isn't industrial competition war—and class strife war ? The principle underlying human struggles is the same, whether it is between countries or individuals. It is time for the National Conscience to awake and put an end to the immorality of Party Government.

RODERICK WENALLT : The man doesn't live who can overthrow Party Government.

LLEWELYN GARTH : If it ought to be done, a way ought to be found to do it.

LORD WENALLT : That's the spirit we want ; and we'll succeed.

RODERICK WENALLT : Ah ! You are bent on taking the plunge, then ?

LORD WENALLT : There will be no plunge. We shall go to work systematically, determinedly, and attack the position with the weapons I understand **Mr.** Garth has suggested. When the people see that his successful factory system has done away with the necessity for strikes, they will begin to realise that business can thrive best without Party trickery.

RODERICK WENALLT : The fireworks of Garth's Factory are not likely to do much—except set the place in a blaze.

LLEWELYN GARTH : There are other weapons, Mr. Wenallt. We shall send all the village fools to Parliament—to represent the folly of the electors.

RODERICK WENALLT (*with a sneer*) : *We* ? (*To* LORD WENALLT) : Is that part of your plan, too ?

LORD WENALLT (*smiling*) : Why not ?

RODERICK WENALLT : The people won't be such fools as to elect them.

LORD WENALLT : They will elect anything with the Party label on. That is the passport to Parliamentary honours.

RODERICK WENALLT : It will be supremely ridiculously.

LLEWELYN GARTH : It's a ridiculous situation.

WILKIN, *attired in a pink coat, canary waistcoat, white top hat, and top boots, a hunting whip in his hand, throws open the door, and coughs to attract attention.* LADY VIOLET *peeps in over his shoulder.*

LLEWELYN GARTH (*points to* WILKIN) : Here is one of our candidates.

RODERICK WENALLT : May I ask what constituency he is going to stand for ?

LORD WENALLT : Not for yours, Roderick, if you come over to us. Otherwise—! It's in your own hands.

RODERICK WENALLT (*with a flash of anger*) : I have to thank you for this, Garth.

LLEWELYN GARTH : You are for the old way. I am for the new. We are at the cross roads, and must separate to fight for our ideals.

RODERICK WENALLT : I accept the challenge.

LADY VIOLET (*with a mischievous smile, pushes* WILKIN *forward*) : Go on, Wilkin.

WILKIN WATKINS : Don't push, my lady, if you please. I don't want to fall and spoil my new clothes.

LORD WENALLT (*laughing*) : Will you join our Party, Mr. Watkins ?

WILKIN WATKINS (*eagerly*) : What Party ? Do you mean a tea party ?

LORD WENALLT : There's always tea on the terrace, and you'll get £400 a year.

WILKIN WATKINS : My goodness ! £400 a year, and wear these clothes ?

LORD WENALLT : That would be part of the bargain.

WILKIN WATKINS : Any poachin' allowed ?

LADY VIOLET : Plenty ! You could make your own laws, and do what you pleased.

WILKIN WATKINS : That is grand—grand ! Is there any work to do ?

LADY VIOLET : No real work ; and you haven't got even to think. You have only got to vote when you are told and how you are told. Oh, Mr. Garth, it is such a lovely idea, and it will be so ridiculous.

LLEWELYN GARTH : I'm glad you approve. Will you canvass for Wilkin ?

LADY VIOLET : Of course, I will.

RODERICK WENALLT (*stiffly*) : Are you going to pay his expenses, my lord ?

LORD WENALLT (*nods*) : Certainly. We call the tune, and must pay the piper. (*After a pause*) : It's worth it. (*Raises his head, and looks thoughtfully at* RODERICK WENALLT, *and then into space, as though he saw his dream taking shape.*) Co-operation in industrial enterprise at home. Co-operation abroad between the peaceful Nations, to restrain and punish the disturbers of the world's peace, and lay the foundation of lasting unity. Why not ? The disputes between Nations are but enlarged editions of the disputes between classes. They shall become things of the past ! and after profitable time spent in the undivided pursuit of our supreme aim, we shall have only one Party—the Party of Patriotism. The voice of Faction shall be silenced, and the stream of our National Life, and the wider stream of International Concord, shall flow with growing volume in an ever-deepening channel of Unified Purpose and of unutterable resolve.

LADY VIOLET (*rapturously*) : Splendid—splendid !

RODERICK WENALLT : Very fine ! But the New Factory ? Are you going to finance that ?

LORD WENALLT : Yes. I give Garth a free hand. All I ask is that the experiment shall not be a failure. It is part of a Great Experiment, Garth, and you must put your heart and soul into it.

LLEWELYN GARTH : It shall not be a failure. There is only one thing that weighs upon my mind. Our success will ruin Jenkin Lewis. I should like to bring him into our scheme.

LORD WENALLT : Do it, if you can. He is a dreadfully obstinate man. I saw him yesterday, but could do nothing with him. I'm afraid there is a very bitter feeling between him and the strikers.

WILKIN WATKINS : As bitter as wormwood. It is a nice cup of tea they are brewing, and they will both have to drink it, the fools ! They are only fit

78

to be members of Parliament—like me and **Mr. Wenallt !** (*chuckles*).

LLEWELYN GARTH : Lady Violet, can't you persuade Jenkin Lewis to join us ?

LADY VIOLET : I can't—I have tried ! But I know what I'll do. I'll work a banner for the New Factory, with the motto : " Co-operation—Unity— Peace "—and march down to the old factory, and coax Jenkin Lewis to " follow the light."

LORD WENALLT (*thoughtfully*) : Co-operation— Unity—Peace ! Yes, child, you shall emblazon those words on **our** banner, and henceforth we'll fight under it (*paces the room in a mood of abstraction*).

LLEWELYN GARTH : You have put our creed into inspiring words, Lady Violet, and I for one will follow the light.

RODERICK WENALLT (*with an ironical laugh*) : I suppose the gentleman who is to oppose me will be your standard-bearer ?

WILKIN WATKINS : Hear, hear ! I will carry it—if it isn't too heavy.

WILKIN *lolls in an easy chair—doses—starts up— doses again.*

LORD WENALLT : The hands that carry the Standard will be ennobled, Roderick.

LADY WENALLT *calls from the door.*

LADY WENALLT : Come and have tea, Wen,

and you, too, Roderick. I'm tired of waiting for you.

RODERICK *crosses to* LADY WENALLT.

RODERICK WENALLT : I'm your man—I want something after the talk I've been listening to.

LADY WENALLT : You'll find your way to the drawing-room, Roderick. (RODERICK *bows and goes out.*)

LADY WENALLT *steps into the room—her eyes leap to* GARTH'S *face.* LORD WENALLT *seems a little anxious.* LADY VIOLET, *smiling to herself, retires into the background.*

LADY WENALLT (*a little agitated—in a low voice*) : Wen ! Who is this ?

LORD WENALLT : My dear, this is **Mr. Garth.** (*Hesitates*) I—I want you to know him (*stands off —watches her with an anxious smile*).

LADY WENALLT (*a little tremulously*) : I am glad to—to see you—**Mr. Garth** (*takes* GARTH'S *hand, holds it long, caressingly*). **Lady Violet** has often spoken to me about you ; so you are not quite —quite a stranger.

LLEWELYN GARTH (*looks about the room like one trying to remember something*) : I don't feel that I am a stranger—although i have no recollection of ever having seen you before—(*with a smile*)— unless it was in a dream.

LADY WENALLT (*watching* GARTH, *with her soul*

in her eyes) : Yes—it must be that—or strangers couldn't feel as though—as though they had known each other always.

LLEWELYN GARTH (*raising his eyes again in a puzzled way to the picture of the child on the wall*) : What a curious thing ! I seem to have seen that picture somewhere. Another dream, I suppose !

LADY WENALLT : Yes—another dream ! You couldn't recollect—No ! You were too young—a mere—

LORD WENALLT (*comes forward quickly—a grave sympathetic smile upon his face*) : Margaret, dear, you look tired. Will you come and rest a little ? I want to talk business with Mr. Garth, and that won't interest you, I'm sure.

LADY WENALLT (*gives her hand to* GARTH, *who helps her to rise from her chair*) : I hope you will come and see me again—soon—Mr. Garth. I shall be thinking of those—dreams—of yours. Some day we may be able to understand them.

LLEWELYN GARTH (*holding the door open for her*) : You have been so kind, Lady Wenallt—I shall be sure to come. (*Looks for consent to* LORD WENALLT, *who nods pleasantly*.)

LORD *and* LADY WENALLT *go out.*

LADY VIOLET (*coming out of the shadows*) : I am so glad you have seen Lady Wenallt, Mr. Garth. She's a dear !

81

upon his shoulder. RODERICK WENALLT *watches her with a cynical, satisfied smile.*

DROP CURTAIN.

A film scene may show the burning factory, excited people clamouring and surging round, gesticulating wildly, their eyes fixed on a window high up in the building, where ARLAIS *is seen through clouds of smoke and flame.* GARTH *rushes upon the scene and saves* ARLAIS.

CURTAIN.

ACT III.

Two Years Later.

—

SCENE.—JENKIN LEWIS' *shop, gloomy and empty, a lamp burning dimly.* ARLAIS, *neatly but drably dressed, is seen standing in the middle of the shop contemplating the empty shelves.* MATTHEW, *more prosperous looking than formerly, comes to the shop door, and glances in doubtfully, uncertain of his welcome. Knocks at the door.*

—

ARLAIS LEWIS : Is it you, Matthew ? It is a long time since you have been here.

MATTHEW JONES (*coming in*) : Yes, indeed—two years to-day.

ARLAIS LEWIS : We don't see many friends since we came down in the world.

MATTHEW JONES : I was thinking it might be like that with you ; so I said to myself—'' The Misses do want a new flannel petticoat, and I will go and get it from the old shop—for the sake of old times.''

ARLAIS LEWIS : It is kind of you to think of us (*with a faint smile and a flash of her old humour*). But, perhaps, you haven't got the quality and the pattern you want—in the New Shop ?

MATTHEW JONES : Don't make any mistake ! You come and see our new shop—big letters over the

85

window, like this—"Co-operation." The employers and workmen are all in one, and divide the profits between them. Oh, we are holding our heads up, now, I can tell you.

ARLAIS LEWIS : And we, here, Matthew, bow our heads before the misfortune that has come upon us.

MATTHEW JONES : You come and live in the New Village, Miss Arlais. It is not a tumble-down old place like this ; but gas in the houses, and big baths, enough to drown yourself in. A bit awkward they were at first, but we get used to them by degrees. And the gardens outside ! Well, you should see the roses and the leeks, and the sunflowers and the onions—everything in season and out of season, too, if you want them.

ARLAIS LEWIS : A pleasant picture you draw, Matthew. You must be very happy in your new homes ?

MATTHEW JONES : Happy ? I should think so. And we have got to thank Llewelyn Garth for it.

ARLAIS LEWIS : How can that be ? He had no money to build such a place. It must have cost thousands.

MATTHEW JONES : Lord Wenallt found the money, and Llewelyn Garth made the plans. It was co-operation between them, and now it is co-operation between us all. And it will last, because it is fair all round. The men are satisfied, because they are not driven to do this and that like mindless beasts ; and Lord Wenallt is satisfied, because he has found a sure way of stopping strikes and keeping trade in the country, and making a bit to put in his pocket as well.

ARLAIS LEWIS (*sadly*) : And the days of prosperity in the Old Village are gone ! My father is too old-fashion to take to the new ways.

MATTHEW JONES : I am sorry in my heart for the old Village. There is something about the place where you were born different to any other place. I often think of the old cottage and the old days at home ; and something pulls at my heart. Ah— well ! I suppose they were just grey milestones left far behind in the old life.

ARLAIS LEWIS : Life is like that, Matthew— patches of all colours. I am glad you haven't torn the Old Village out of your heart.

MATTHEW JONES : No, indeed. And there is our New Chapel. It is very grand, but it is not like the Old Chapel. The smell of the paint is different to me ; and the place is so big, and the Minister is so small, that you can't help thinking more of the building than the pastor. In the old chapel there was a little crack in the window by the place where I used to sit, and through it the wind used to whisper

87

to me when the sermon was over, and tell me to wake up.

ARLAIS LEWIS : Oh, Matthew !

MATTHEW JONES (*smiling*) : Very wicked, wasn't it ? And I had another friend there, too—a big old spider, always in the corner over my head. The sermon didn't trouble him. There he was watching for flies, and drawing them into his net ; and it made me think of the masters drawing the workmen into *their* net, and tangling them up until they had no freedom. Ah—well ! I only want a bit of red flannel.

JENKIN LEWIS *looks across from the parlour door at* MATTHEW, *a deep frown on his pale, drawn face.* MATTHEW *and* ARLAIS *have their backs towards him.*

ARLAIS LEWIS : There is nothing in the shop, Matthew—not even a yard of floor cloth. There is no factory and no business since the fire.

MATTHEW JONES : My ! it was an awful fire. I could see it in my dreams for months—and you in the top window. You 'ouldn't be here now, but for Llewelyn Garth. Great God ! It was a grand sight. And your father has never given him a word of thanks. Oh, he is a hard man.

ARLAIS LEWIS : He can't bring himself to forgive Garth. But he is very tender to me.

MATTHEW JONES : Well—well ! that is how

he is made, I suppose. It is a pity for him, too. I don't like to see him go down.

JENKIN LEWIS (*coming into the shop*) : If you didn't want to see me go down, why did you set fire to my Factory ?

MATTHEW JONES (*startled*) : Me set fire to your Factory ! In the name of God ! what are you saying ?

JENKIN LEWIS : I am saying the truth. Why did you do it ?

MATTHEW JONES : Look here, Mr. Lewis, I am not the sort of man to do a thing like that. You remember that, or there'll be trouble.

JENKIN LEWIS : It was you or Llewelyn Garth.

ARLAIS LEWIS : Father ! don't—don't say that.

MATTHEW JONES : There is not much odds what you say about me and the other fellows, but, look you, Jenkin Lewis, you had better leave Llewelyn Garth alone.

JENKIN LEWIS : It is strange to hear a workman defending the man that is over him.

MATTHEW JONES : We have got cause to defend him. But for him, where should we be to-day ? Slaving for you and men like you, year in and year out, and never a shilling saved for our old age.

JENKIN LEWIS : There is the old age pension. What more do you want ?

against me for the J.P. A snake in the grass, that's what he is.

ARLAIS LEWIS (*a little nervously*) : And Llewelyn Garth has been here, too.

JENKIN LEWIS : He is the worst of the lot. It is through him we are brought to this—(*sweeps his arm round to indicate the empty shop*). If it hadn't been for him, the men would have given in.

ARLAIS LEWIS : He tried hard to bring you and the men together, but you wouldn't listen.

JENKIN LEWIS : If it hadn't been for the New Factory, the men would have given in.

ARLAIS LEWIS : Yes—given in to starvation, but not to reason. Such a peace couldn't last. Llewelyn Garth knew that, and tried to make the Old Factory what the New Factory is now.

JENKIN LEWIS : He took the bread out of my mouth.

ARLAIS LEWIS : Oh, why will you shut your eyes to the truth ? Use your reason, father, and see things as they are. The world is moving on, and those who stand still are left behind. Let me send for Garth——

JENKIN LEWIS : What do you want him for ? Is he anything to you ?

ARLAIS LEWIS : He is my friend, and is yours, too, in spite of what you say.

JENKIN LEWIS : I won't have him coming here.

ARLAIS LEWIS : Then there is nothing for me to do but go and earn my living.

JENKIN LEWIS : What are you talking about ! I suppose it is that fellow, Garth, that has been putting such nonsense in your head ? Don't let me hear any more about it. (JACOB MORGAN *looks in from the shop door*.) Here is another snake, Jacob. I 'on't see him (*moves away quickly towards the parlour door*).

JACOB MORGAN (*coming into the shop quickly*) : Oh-ho ! Running away, are you, Jenkin Lewis ?

JENKIN LEWIS (*facing* JACOB MORGAN *sharply*) : Not from a man like you, if you are a J.P.

JACOB MORGAN : I am only a J.P. when I am trying cases, and at present you are trying me. You are a very trying man, friend Jenkin. You will want a special place made for you in the next world. (*Deposits a brown paper parcel on the counter, and whispers to* ARLAIS) : A few groceries for you, merchi.

JENKIN LEWIS (*sharply*) : What is that parcel you are bringing here ?

JACOB MORGAN : It is a parcel. I am just resting it for a minute on the counter.

JENKIN LEWIS *grunts, and turns away towards the parlour.*

JACOB MORGAN : You are in a great hurry, Jenkin Lewis. Not so fast, please ! I have got a little bill for you in my pocket (*fumbles in his pocket*).

JENKIN LEWIS (*turns back slowly*) : I can't pay it ; the bailiffs have been here before you, and taken everything I had.

JACOB MORGAN : That is unfortunate. But, you see, I must have money to carry on my business.

WILKIN, *in top boots, white hat, and fur-lined coat, shuffles in, followed by a quaint-looking boy, DAVIE, a personal servant.*

JACOB MORGAN (*bows elaborately to WILKIN*) : Well-I-never ! if here isn't our new Member. I hope I see you well, Mr. Watkins ?

JENKIN LEWIS *sits down moodily, and reads a paper.*

WILKIN WATKINS : Wilkin Watkins, Esquire, M.P., if you please. Here is my card (*hands card*). I am famous, thank you, Mr. J.P. (*chuckles*). How are you, Mr. Lewis ? (JENKIN LEWIS *ruffles his paper, and turns his back to WILKIN.*) Getting a bit deaf, I s'pose. How are you, Miss Arlais ?

ARLAIS LEWIS : We are in great trouble, Wilkin.

WILKIN WATKINS : Oh, that's a pity. Come you, trouble dies of old age, like everything else. Davie ! take my coat off, and don't tumble it.

DAVIE (*very quick*) : Yes, sir (*takes WILKIN'S coat—stands stiffly upright, the coat across his arm*).

WILKIN WATKINS : Davie ! give me my silk

94

pocket handkerchief, with the M.P. in the corner. (DAVIE *gives handkerchief from coat pocket.*) **Drat it !** I don't like this business. It is Lord Wenallt's doing. He says every M.P. must have a servant, a bath every day, and behave like an advertiser—to keep the eyes of the public on him. And Davie is dressing me as I was never dressed before. I don't like it ; but I have got to do it, haven't I, Davie ?

DAVIE : Yes, sir. Them's his lordship's orders.

WILKIN WATKINS : Splendid memory you have got, Davie. Which Party do you belong to, Davie ?

DAVIE : The £400-a-year-Party, sir—so long as it lasts.

ARLAIS *laughs.*

WILKIN WATKINS (*with a wink*) : You mustn't make fun of old Wilkin, or he'll report you to the Speaker (*chuckles*).

ARLAIS LEWIS : I thought Members of Parliament were all serious, elderly gentlemen, not given to joking.

WILKIN WATKINS : They are all jokers in Parliament, ain't they, Davie ?

DAVIE : Yes, sir.

WILKIN WATKINS : If I said they were all devils—(*jurking his thumb towards* DAVIE, *and chuckling*)—he'd say the same.

DAVIE : Yes, sir.

WILKIN WATKINS : And if I said they were all angels, he'd say——

DAVIE : No, sir—I couldn't go so far as that.

WILKIN WATKINS : I have been writing a catechism for Davie (*opens a pocket-book—glances at it and then at* DAVIE) : What does M.P. stand for, Davie ?

DAVIE : Much Pay—little profit—to the people.

WILKIN WATKINS : Right ! What does P.M. stand for, Davie ?

DAVIE : Post Mortem on the country after death caused by Party Quacks.

WILKIN WATKINS : Right ! What is the motto for to-day, Davie ?

DAVIE (*glances at almanac*) : Seventeenth day of the month—Do, lest you be done.

WILKIN WATKINS : Wrong ! (*chuckles*). That is the motto for every day.

DAVIE (*glances at almanac again*) : Beg pardon, sir. Do nothing to-day that somebody else will do for you to-morrow.

WILKIN WATKINS : Right ! When the Chancellor walked the tight rope between Chilly and the other place, what did the Prime Minister say, Davie ?

DAVIE : Don't know, sir. I haven't got as far as that yet.

WILKIN WATKINS : I am ashamed of you. " Balancing again, are you ?" That's what he

said. (JENKIN LEWIS *grunts loudly and rattles his paper*.) We shall make Mr. Lewis as human as the people across the North Sea, if we make him laugh like this, Davie. You are looking as prosperous as ever, Jacob Morgan. How is business ?

JACOB MORGAN : Business has left the Old Village, and gone to the New. I shall have to strike or supply goods on the Good Samaritan principle.

WILKIN WATKINS : Good Samaritan is best. The men of the New Factory will burn your house down if you strike. And who 'ould make the coffins for the people then ? They will die, strike or no strike, and there is no undertaker in the village but you. You can't die nor strike 'till you find somebody to take your place.

JACOB MORGAN : Just so, Mr. Watkins. But perhaps you are not aware that the Doctor is on strike ?

WILKIN WATKINS : Oh, well, if he is on strike, perhaps they 'on't want any coffins for a bit (*chuckles—looks round the shop*). The shop is very empty, Jenkin Lewis ; and you don't look very full yourself.—Davie !

DAVIE (*at attention*) : Yes, sir ?

WILKIN WATKINS (*turns his back to* DAVIE) : Put on my coat—(DAVIE *putting the coat on himself*) —and don't tear the linings. Seal-skin made out of rabbits it is (*turns his head*). Well, there's a fool for you ! Put it on me, your master. (DAVIE *hurriedly slips out of the coat*), not on you, you monkey.

DAVIE : Beg pardon, sir (*helps* WILKIN *on with his coat*).

WILKIN WATKINS : I should think so. It isn't for you 'till I have been in the gutter a few times. Come on, Davie. (*To* ARLAIS) : I will be back in a minute.

WILKIN *trots out, followed by* DAVIE.

JENKIN LEWIS : You can go, too, Jacob Morgan. I haven't got any money for you.

JACOB MORGAN (*slowly approaches* JENKIN LEWIS, *with a kindly smile*) : I didn't come here for money, Jenkin Lewis, but just in a neighbourly way to see how you were getting on.

ARLAIS *sits down, takes up some sewing, listens eagerly.*

JENKIN LEWIS (*fiercely*): Can't you leave me alone?

JACOB MORGAN : I am thinking what you would do if I was in great trouble and left to shift for myself, with nothing in my pocket. You wouldn't let principle stand between you and a man in misfortune, would you ? Answer me truly, Jenkin Lewis, and, remember, the Almighty will hear you —if you tell a lie.

JENKIN LEWIS (*after a struggle*) : It 'ould be my duty to help you—in spite of your J.P.

THE GREAT EXPERIMENT

JACOB MORGAN (*smiling*) : I knew you would say that.   You have got a good heart, but a stubborn head, Jenkin Lewis.   There has never been anything between us but two letters of the alphabet, and I would never have touched them, if I had known they would make bad blood between us.   As it is, it would suit us both better to have A.S.S. after our names than anything else.

JENKIN LEWIS : Do you mean that, Jacob Morgan ?

JACOB MORGAN : I am not a joker like Wilkin Watkins.   If we can't be good friends in prosperity, we can be good friends in adversity, and help one another a bit.   That is my feeling, Jenkin Lewis.

JENKIN LEWIS *gets up, his eyes search* JACOB MORGAN'S *face—they shake hands silently.*   JENKIN LEWIS *slowly turns away, and, with almost a sob of awakened feeling, goes out of the room.*

ARLAIS LEWIS (*throws down her sewing, springs to her feet, her eyes glistening—seizes* JACOB MORGAN'S *hand, and presses it in both of hers.*)   Oh, I'm so glad—so glad !

JACOB MORGAN : There are not too many of the old brigade left, and they shouldn't quarrel, and set a bad example to the young ones.

ARLAIS LEWIS : You will stand by him !   You will, won't you ?

JACOB MORGAN : You can be sure of that. But why are you so anxious. ?

ARLAIS LEWIS : I may have to go away.

JACOB MORGAN : Name-of-goodness ! What for ?

ARLAIS LEWIS : I must do something—I must earn my living. You will come and see him often —when I am away ?

JACOB MORGAN : Indeed I will—if you must go. Your father is a strange man, and I am a strange man, and I suppose that is why we have been strange to one another. But from this time out we are going to be friends. And, remember, you are always welcome to anything I have got in my shop, pay or no pay, so long as I can keep it open.

ARLAIS LEWIS : Thank you—thank you ! But it is hard to accept charity from anyone who isn't near to us.

JACOB MORGAN (*with a whimsical smile*) : Am I not near to you ? I may not be a relation—but there is only a few inches between us.

WILKIN *shuffles in, followed by* DAVIE, *who is carrying a large paper parcel.*

WILKIN WATKINS (*chuckling*) : We have been helping ourselves in your shop, J.P.—haven't we, Davie ?

DAVIE : Yes, sir ; and the gentleman will find a sovereign on the counter to pay for the goods.

THE GREAT EXPERIMENT

WILKIN WATKINS : Davie is very honest.   He always pays for things out of my money.   Put the parcel on the counter, Davie.

DAVIE :   Yes, sir (*deposits the parcel on the counter*).

WILKIN WATKINS (*holds his nose*) :   Mind don't break the eggs.   A few things for you and your father, Miss Arlais—a present from Wilkin and Davie, General Confiscators.

ARLAIS LEWIS :   It is kind of you, very kind ; but I really can't take anything.   Father wouldn't let me.

WILKIN WATKINS :   It isn't take, it's give. You pay me £400 a year out of the taxes, and this is a bit of discount.   (*In a confidential undertone*) : If it is moonlight to-night, I will go and catch a hare for you, and give the old gentleman a good feed. You shall come with me, J.P.   You are a dab-hand at catching rabbits.   Davie shall keep watch—'on't you, Davie ?

DAVIE :   Yes, sir.   I'm a weasel at watching. I can smell a keeper a mile off.

WILKIN WATKINS :   Yes—a rotten one, I s'pose (*pulling* JACOB *towards the door*).   Come on, mun !   A J.P. and M.P. together will frighten all the rabbits in the parish into the nets.   If we see old Roderick Wenallt, we will put him in the river (*chuckles*).

101

JACOB MORGAN (*laughing—from the door*) : Good-night, Arlais. The ways of Wilkin Watkins are strange ! You will hear of us in the Police Court next, I expect.

ARLAIS, *smiling in spite of herself, watches them out, and then puts up the shutters, and closes the shop door. In a few moments the door is opened, and* GARTH *comes in.* ARLAIS *sees him, tip-toes to the parlour door, her finger on her lips, and closes it softly, then crosses to* GARTH.

ARLAIS LEWIS : I don't want Father to know you are here. I have pleaded with him, but it's no use.

LLEWELYN GARTH : I am sorry. Why, the place is empty !

ARLAIS LEWIS : The bailiffs have taken everything.

LLEWELYN GARTH (*distressed*) : This is bad, indeed.

ARLAIS LEWIS : It was dreadful to see them carrying away mother's arm-chair. Father is nearly broken-hearted about it. And they have taken my piano.

LLEWELYN GARTH : Who put the bailiffs in ?

ARLAIS LEWIS : The Bank—I think it was.

LLEWELYN GARTH (*slowly—fixing his eyes upon* ARLAIS) : Why didn't Mr. Wenallt stop it ? He is one of the directors.

102

ARLAIS LEWIS (*hastily*) : He couldn't—he told me so.

LLEWELYN GARTH : Don't believe him. He is putting pressure on your father—God knows what for.

ARLAIS LEWIS : You have no business to say that.

LLEWELYN GARTH : I am sorry you defend him. I had hoped you were not so friendly.

ARLAIS LEWIS : You are prejudiced against him —as much as father is against you.

LLEWELYN GARTH : No, Arlais, I am not prejudiced—I am anxious—on your account (*a pause*). Since the day of the fire, when I carried you in my arms, I have felt that I had almost a brother's right to stand between you and harm. My regard for you compels me to warn you against Mr. Wenallt.

ARLAIS LEWIS : You don't know how kind he has been. He is going to do a lot for father. He has promised to re-build the factory—when—when— (*looks down nervously—blushes*)—after—(*pauses*).

LLEWELYN GARTH : After what ? (ARLAIS *is silent.*) What price are *you* going to pay Mr. Wenallt for his promised favours ?

ARLAIS LEWIS : I don't understand you.

LLEWELYN GARTH : It's as well you don't. You know he's engaged to Lady Violet ?

103

ARLAIS LEWIS : That isn't true. He told me it isn't true.

LLEWELYN GARTH : If he told you that, he lied to you—deceived you intentionally.

ARLAIS LEWIS : How dare you say that !

LLEWELYN GARTH : I dare say it, because it's true. Mr. Wenallt *is* engaged to Lady Violet, and he'll never give her up. Her wealth and position are necessary to him. Remember that, Arlais, and don't let him make a fool of you.

ARLAIS LEWIS (*smiles confidently*) : Would *you* marry for wealth and position ?

LLEWELYN GARTH : That is beside the question.

ARLAIS LEWIS (*stamps her foot*) : Would you ?

LLEWELYN GARTH : No—not for those things only.

ARLAIS LEWIS : Then, why should he ?

LLEWELYN GARTH : Our positions are different. I am one of the people—free to consult my own feelings, and indifferent to the ban of Society. He is Lord Wenallt's nearest male relative—stands in the place of a son. He is not the man to forfeit his uncle's good-will for the sake of sentiment. You will be placed in the scale against power and wealth, and human nature being what it is, you can't be sure that you will weigh the heaviest.

ARLAIS LEWIS : Don't you think Lady Violet

will have something to say to this arrangement ? Suppose she loves someone else ?

LLEWELYN GARTH : I can't suppose anything of the sort. Her marriage with Mr. Wenallt is a family arrangement, and she will marry him from a sense of duty.

ARLAIS LEWIS (*smiles into* GARTH'S *face*) : You silly Garth ! I know her better than you do. She will never marry Mr. Wenallt.

LLEWELYN GARTH : You are talking about what you don't understand.

ARLAIS LEWIS : It is true all the same. Nobody has guessed it but me—not even (*looking straight at* GARTH) the man most concerned. I think he is a little blind. She is very beautiful, Mr. Blind Bat.

LLEWELYN GARTH : It is well for our peace-of-mind to be blind to things beyond our reach. She is too beautiful, too exalted, for a nameless man to think about—except in a dream.

ARLAIS LEWIS : Dreams sometimes come true.

LLEWELYN GARTH : I hope, dear girl, *your* dream may come true ; but I'm terribly afraid. Take care of yourself until I return.

ARLAIS LEWIS : Are you going away ?

LLEWELYN GARTH : Only for a week's holiday to town. I called to give you this (*hands her an envelope.*)

105

ARLAIS LEWIS : What is it ?

LLEWELYN GARTH : A little present (*pushes it into her hands*).

ARLAIS LEWIS : It is very kind of you (*takes the present—he holds her hands.*) It is nice to feel that one has friends in the dark days.

LLEWELYN GARTH : Good-bye, Arlais.

ARLAIS LEWIS : Good-bye, Garth. You will always think of me kindly, whatever happens ?

LLEWELYN GARTH : Always, Arlais, always ! If you were my sister—(*smiles*)—I should seal my promise with a kiss ; but as you are a wilful Girton girl, it's just " Good-bye !"

ARLAIS LEWIS (*smiling mischievously*) : Good-bye, Garth (*drops his hand*), my brother ! (*runs away with a laugh, and watches him from the parlour door going out into the street. She opens the envelope—takes out a bank note—stares at it.*) Ten pounds ! Dear Garth ! (*Opens the parlour door and calls " Father ! Father ! Where are you ?" Runs into the parlour, and comes out again.*) I forgot ! It's Club night. (*Sighs—sits down—stares into the fire—her back towards the shop door.*)

GARTH *re-enters—steals up behind* ARLAIS—*puts his hands over her eyes—playfully.*)

ARLAIS LEWIS (*with a little start*) : Is it you, Roderick ?

RODERICK WENALLT *stands at the shop door un-*

observed, his eyes fixed on GARTH *and* ARLAIS (GARTH *drops his hands*).

ARLAIS (*turns round—sees* GARTH) : Oh, it's you, Garth. I thought—(*stops—confused*).

GARTH (*coldly*) : I forgot to tell you, Lady Violet would like to see you at the Castle to-morrow.

ARLAIS LEWIS : I—I should like to see her, but I—I'm not sure that it will be possible——

RODERICK WENALLT (*coughs—comes into the shop*) : I'm sorry to interrupt such an interesting tete-a-tete. I, too, have a message for Miss Lewis, but I don't think it would interest Mr. Garth.

LLEWELYN GARTH (*to* ARLAIS) : What answer shall I give Lady Violet ?

ARLAIS LEWIS (*hesitates—looks at* RODERICK WENALLT) : Tell her—tell her—I have other plans for to-morrow. (GARTH *bows coldly*.)

LLEWELYN GARTH : I am on my way to the Castle, Mr. Wenallt. Have you any message to send to Lady Violet ?

RODERICK WENALLT : I always carry my own messages to that quarter, thank you.

LLEWELYN GARTH : I thought she might be interested to know that I had met you here to-night.

RODERICK WENALLT : Her cousinly solicitude is quite natural, Mr. Garth. By all means, relieve

107

her anxiety, and tell her I am in good company. I shall not forget the favour, believe me.

LLEWELYN GARTH : Nor shall I forget the occasion.

GARTH *turns on his heel and goes out quickly.* RODERICK WENALLT *locks the street door, and pulls down the blinds.*

RODERICK WENALLT : Thank goodness ! he's gone.

ARLAIS LEWIS (*with a sigh*) : I wish you and Garth would get on better together.

RODERICK WENALLT : You mustn't expect the impossible. Do you suppose I can forgive him for turning me out of Parliament and putting that fool, Wilkin, in my place ? Why, he's made me the laughing-stock of the county. And there's Lord Wenallt—bitten mad with the fellow's impossible schemes. His name and his factory and his follies are on everybody's lips. He's discussed seriously in Parliament even. Old friends quarrel over him ; and the Party System is shaken to its foundation. Half my friends are out ; and village clowns have taken their place, and deal with affairs of State as though they were selling goods over the counter.

ARLAIS LEWIS : Have you come here to quarrel with me about Garth ?

RODERICK WENALLT (*pulls up short—forces a*

smile) : Of course not. I've come here to keep my promise (*takes her in his arm—kisses her*).

ARLAIS LEWIS (*looking round nervously*) : If father saw you !

RODERICK WENALLT : Don't you think he would approve of me as a son-in-law ? (*she hides her face on his shoulder*). But he won't see me. He's safe at the Oddfellow's Club. (*Notices envelope in* ARLAIS' *hand*) What's that ?

ARLAIS LEWIS (*disengaging herself—shows bank note*) : It's a present from Garth.

RODERICK WENALLT (*takes note—reads the number—thinks rapidly*) : Does he often give you presents ?

ARLAIS LEWIS : Not often. But he is going away for a holiday ; and I think he wants to be kind to father.

RODERICK WENALLT : Yes, I know—he's going to-night. I make it my business to know Mr. Garth's movements. I shall catch him tripping some day. £10 ! He must be very fond of you.

ARLAIS LEWIS : Don't be ridiculous !

RODERICK WENALLT : I don't like other people giving you presents. You must let me change this note for you. If you take it to the bank yourself, they would know you got it from Garth.

ARLAIS LEWIS : How could they know that ?

RODERICK WENALLT : They keep the numbers

109

of all the notes passed over the counter, and can always trace them.

ARLAIS LEWIS : Well, what if they do ? I don't mind.

RODERICK WENALLT : But I mind. I don't want those cackling clerks to think that you are on such intimate terms with Garth.

ARLAIS LEWIS (*smiling*) : Oh ! (RODERICK WENALLT *puts the note in his pocket.*) I want— (*holds out her hand*)—the cash, please.

RODERICK WENALLT (*raises her hand to his lips*) : That's the only coin you'll get from me until to-morrow. After that, Mrs. Roderick Wenallt will have a banking account of her own to draw upon.

ARLAIS LEWIS : Shall I really—(*looking up at him wistfully*)—really be Mrs. Roderick Wenallt— to-morrow ? (RODERICK WENALLT *nods.*) It seems like a dream !

RODERICK WENALLT : A dream ? Umph ! Have you packed your things ?

ARLAIS LEWIS : Yes.

RODERICK WENALLT (*links his arm in hers*) : Then we'd better be off before the old man returns.

ARLAIS LEWIS (*hangs back, reluctant to go— pleadingly*) : Wait a minute, Roderick, only a minute. I—I can't go without wishing father good-bye.

RODERICK WENALLT : Then you won't go

ACT IV.

Six Months Later.

—

SCENE.—*The Library at Wenallt Castle. Balcony showing through open French window at the back. Trees and grounds beyond.*

As the curtain rises, the FOOTMAN *is seen putting up flags, emblazoned with the emblem, " Co-operation—Unity—Peace "—in gold letters.* GARTH *comes in, carrying a bundle of letters in his hand.*

—

LLEWELYN GARTH : Hullo ! What are you doing that for, Williams ?

FOOTMAN : Dont' know, sir. His lordship's orders.

LLEWELYN GARTH : Oh, look here, you know very well. Tell me, what's the business ?

FOOTMAN : Not knowing, can't say, sir. But I expect it's a political gathering of some sort in the grounds. The cook's made a lot of preparations— if that's any criterion. It's my experience, sir, that a crowd is never wantin' when there's a feast on the table. Ahem ! excuse me, sir. (*Exit.*)

GARTH *sits down at the desk in the middle of the room, and reads the letters, making memoranda as he reads.*

LADY VIOLET *enters silently, stops for a moment*

115

near the door, unseen by GARTH, *and regards him with a smile he would have given much to see.*

LADY VIOLET : Good morning, Mr. Garth.

LLEWELYN GARTH (*rises*) : Good morning, Lady Violet.

LADY VIOLET : Shall I interfere with you very much if I write a letter on that—(*points to the opposite side of the writing table*)—side of the table ?

LLEWELYN GARTH : Not at all (*places a chair for her.*)

LADY VIOLET (*looking him in the face demurely*) : Thank you ! (*seats herself*).

GARTH *goes slowly back to his chair, sits down, and in an abstracted way contemplates the pile of letters before him, moves them about aimlessly, and occasionally lifts his eyes to watch* LADY VIOLET *as she sketches his face, unsuspected by him.*)

LADY VIOLET (*catching his eyes bent upon her, he is a little confused. She smiles*) : You don't appear to be getting on very well with your work, Mr. Secretary Garth.

LLEWELYN GARTH : No—I'm afraid not. My mind wanders into forbidden ways, and refuses to be interested in the commonplace.

LADY VIOLET : That's awkward. I have suffered from the same thing myself, and can sympathise with you. Forbidden things are always so tantalising.

116

LLEWELYN GARTH : Yes ; and they seem so near sometimes—so near that they seem to call out to you to raise your arms and grasp them for your own. Then you awake—the vision fades—and you realise that your imagination has cheated you.

LADY VIOLET : But you have had your vision. It's delightful to be able to imagine things.

LLEWELYN GARTH : Not those things that are unattainable.

LADY VIOLET : Oh ! I should have thought that a first rate imagination would lift us above difficulties.

LLEWELYN GARTH : But, if you are forbidden to raise your arms to grasp the thing you want, how can imagination help you ?

LADY VIOLET : If I were a man, I don't think I should imagine that. I should raise my arms, and take what I wanted.

LLEWELYN GARTH : That is what Adam did, and paid the penalty.

LADY VIOLET : Oh, that was a long time ago— in the unsophisticated age. You have been more fortunate than Adam. You have raised your arms to grasp success, and you have grasped it. You have done what you set out to do. The great meeting to be held here to-day is a tribute to your success.

LLEWELYN GARTH : Oh, that's it ! I didn't

understand. But what you call my success I owe to Lord Wenallt.

LADY VIOLET : That is curious. He told me that the progress he has made in his great scheme is largely due to you.

LLEWELYN GARTH : He is too kind. I am merely the instrument his fingers play upon.

LADY VIOLET : The instrument is as necessary as the fingers, don't you think ?

LLEWELYN GARTH : It's generous of you to put it that way.

LADY VIOLET : You are both extremely modest men. But, really, *you* are such a wise, venerable old man, you know—you inspire confidence even in me ! (*laughs*). Twenty-nine to-day, aren't you ?

LLEWELYN GARTH : Yes. A birthday is not a very important event in the life of a nameless man.

LADY VIOLET : A nameless man has the privilege of making a name for himself. I think this is going to be an eventful day for you.

LLEWELYN GARTH : An eventful day ? Why ? What is going to happen ?

LADY VIOLET : I don't know ! but there's something in the air. I have seen Lord and Lady Wenallt nodding and smiling mysteriously together, and whispering your name in the most tantalising way. I asked them to tell me what it all meant, but they shook their heads, and told me not to be

118

curious. Now, you are as wise as I am. We are both in the same boat, Mr. Garth—the boat of uncertainty.

LLEWELYN GARTH (*looking at her*) : There's room for hope in uncertainty, isn't there ?

LADY VIOLET (*thoughtfully*) : There may be— yes, I think there is (*their eyes meet, and flash an understanding*).

LADY VIOLET *moves towards the door, stops half way, turns to* GARTH *with an affectionate gesture.*

LADY VIOLET : Shall I tell Lady Wenallt ?

LLEWELYN GARTH : Yes ! let us be above board.

LADY VIOLET : Thank you for saying that. (*She adds sweetly, as she lowers her eyes*) : **Garth !**

GARTH *rises impulsively. She makes a little step towards him, shyly, but smiling still.*

LLEWELYN GARTH : Don't—don't tempt me, or I shall forget everything but that I love you.

LADY VIOLET : I hope you'll never forget that. (*Again the sweet, musical invitation in her voice*) : **Garth !**

GARTH *springs to her side and kisses her. She disengages herself slowly, gently, and flies to the door, with a happy laugh. The* FOOTMAN *throws it open, and announces "* MR. RODERICK WENALLT," *who walks in with an assured smile. (Exit* FOOTMAN.)

RODERICK WENALLT : Ah ! Violet, I needn't

ask how you are.   You are looking as charming as a blushing rose.

LADY VIOLET (*a little confused*) : A-a-am I ?

RODERICK WENALLT (*laughs, turns away, nods to* GARTH) : Morning, Mr. Garth. I thought you were in London.   You often disappear, don't you ? The Lewis girl has disappeared, too. A peculiar coincidence, isn't it ? A deuced pretty girl, don't you think ? I admire Garth's taste, immensely, Violet.

LLEWELYN GARTH (*quietly*) : I think you would admire it more (*with a glance at* LADY VIOLET) if you knew a little more about it. As you appear to take an interest in my movements, Mr. Wenallt, I may inform you that my visits to London are matters of business (*looking at him straight*) not pleasure.

RODERICK WENALLT : Of course, business— private business—to consult the Authorities on petti- coat government—what ?

FOOTMAN *enters hurriedly.*

FOOTMAN : If you please, Lady Violet, her lady- ship would like to see you at once.

LADY VIOLET : Is she alone ? (*moving to door.*)

FOOTMAN : Yes, my lady.

RODERICK WENALLT : Come back soon, Violet. I want to see you.

LADY VIOLET (*with 'a laugh*) : I fancy I shall

have a lot to say (*turning to* GARTH *with a smile*) to
Lady Wenallt. Don't expect me 'till you see me.

LADY VIOLET *goes out, followed by the* FOOTMAN.

LLEWELYN GARTH (*swings round and faces*
RODERICK WENALLT *with a stern face*) : I shall be
obliged, Mr. Wenallt, if you will not in future place
me in an equivocal position by unfounded insinua-
tions.

RODERICK WENALLT : My dear fellow, I only
repeat common gossip.

LLEWELYN GARTH : Then common gossip
lies, and you know it.

RODERICK WENALLT (*with assumed indig-
nation*) : Mr. Garth !—I'm willing to make allow-
ance for you, but I'm damned if I'll put up with your
impertinence.

LADY VIOLET *re-enters quickly. She looks from
one to the other, draws in her breath sharply.*

RODERICK WENALLT : You didn't stop
long.

LADY VIOLET : No (*looks at* GARTH). Jacob
Morgan has just come in to see Lady Wenallt, and I
couldn't tell her what I wanted to. Mr. Garth, do
you mind taking your letters into another room for a
few minutes ? (GARTH *gathers up letters.*) I have
something to say to Mr. Wenallt. Do you mind ?

LLEWELYN GARTH : Oh, no (*moving to
door—turns, and looks at* RODERICK WENALLT).

121

I shall have something to say to Mr. Wenallt, too (*goes out*).

RODERICK WENALLT : Really, this young man is quite melodramatic ! Why on earth should you ask him if he minded what you said or did ? It is no concern of his.

LADY VIOLET : Is it any concern of yours ? (*Sharply*) What did you mean, Roderick, by what you said just now—about Arlais Lewis ?

RODERICK WENALLT : My dear Violet, let us discuss something more pleasant than other people's follies. Suppose we discuss ourselves ? I'm tired of Garth and the factory girl.

LADY VIOLET : I hate to hear you speak of the poor girl in that cold-blooded way. I should like to know what has become of her.

RODERICK WENALLT : Then you had better ask Garth.

LADY VIOLET : Why should I ask Garth ?

RODERICK WENALLT : Don't you usually go for information to people who know ?

LADY VIOLET : Yes—that is why I thought I'd come to you.

RODERICK WENALLT : You've made a bad shot this time.

LADY VIOLET : Perhaps so. But I mean to get at the truth.

RODERICK WENALLT : Certainly. I'll help

122

you in that laudable object, but not now. Forget the girl for a moment. I want to talk to you about our plans for the future. It's quite time I settled down, don't you think ?

LADY VIOLET : If you want my candid opinion, I think you are too unstable, too fond of the world and its pleasures, ever to settle down.

RODERICK WENALLT : Oh, come, I'm as tame as a canary. You are horribly tantalising ! Be kind for once, and put an end to my bachelor days. I'll give you a good time, I promise you—ever so much better than wasting your time amongst the village rustics.

LADY VIOLET : I am very fond of village rustics, and quite contented as I am. You mustn't feel hurt, Roderick, if I tell you to think less of me and more of —someone else.

RODERICK WENALLT : You say that—after knowing me all these years !

LADY VIOLET : Don't you think that may be the reason ?

RODERICK WENALLT (*looking at her intently*) : You have another reason ?

LADY VIOLET (*hesitatingly*) : Possibly.

RODERICK WENALLT : Ah ! (*picks up the sketch of* GARTH LADY VIOLET *had left on the table, looks at it, and then at her.*) A clever sketch of Garth—very. Did you do it ?

LADY VIOLET : Yes—in an idle moment. Will you put it back, please ?

RODERICK WENALLT (*puts the sketch back on the table, with slow deliberation.*) A very clever sketch ; but rather idealised, don't you think ?

LADY VIOLET : Idealised ? No, I don't think so.

RODERICK WENALLT (*glancing at her, with a queer smile*): Perhaps I should have said " idolised ?"

LADY VIOLET : A critic may say what he pleases. Sometimes he's right ; sometimes he's wrong.

RODERICK WENALLT : You don't contradict me.

LADY VIOLET : A critic is above contradiction.

RODERICK WENALLT : You are clever. You make me more than ever in love with you. (LADY VIOLET *bites her lips—turns away from him.*) Do you know, I'm a little bit surprised that you should be on such intimate terms with a fellow in Garth's equivocal position.

LADY VIOLET (*faces round suddenly*): Equivocal ? That's another wrong word, Roderick. Mr. Garth is my father's private secretary. I have the greatest respect for him ; and I should consider it an honour—to bear his name. After such a confession, will you hold me to the arrangement made for us by our relatives ?

RODERICK WENALLT (*chagrined—tries to hide*

124

it) : I don't hold you to anything. (*A pause.*) You asked me just now what had become of Arlais Lewis. I didn't want to tell you.   I wanted to shield Garth.

LADY VIOLET : You would—naturally. You have always shown a great affection for him. But, what has he to do with Arlais Lewis ?

RODERICK WENALLT : I'm going to tell you. You remember the night the girl disappeared ?

LADY VIOLET (*impatiently*) : Of course I remember.

RODERICK WENALLT (*slowly—watching her*) : That same night Garth visited her at her father's house, secretly, after dark, and gave her money.

LADY VIOLET (*sharply*) : Well, what of that ? They were old friends.

RODERICK WENALLT : Something more than old friends. (*Shows bank note*) This is one of the notes he gave her. He got it from the Bank—the number was taken down—and the girl cashed it. That night he went away.   They were seen together in London.

LADY VIOLET : I can't believe it—I won't believe it.   You are slandering Mr. Garth.

RODERICK WENALLT : After daring to raise his eyes to you, it does seem a damned insolent thing to have done.

LADY VIOLET : Really, Roderick ! you forget yourself.

RODERICK WENALLT : I don't want to strain anything against him, but when I look back, and remember things, I've no doubt about what I've told you. Ever since he saved her from the fire, he's been dangling about the shop—when the old man's back was turned.

LADY VIOLET : I don't want to hear any more.

RODERICK WENALLT : But I've got to tell you, now I've begun. It's better for you to know the truth. Why did he worry my uncle into employing Jenkin Lewis,—if it wasn't for the girl's sake—to ease his conscience, and that sort of thing ?

LADY VIOLET (*distressed*) : Oh ! it seems impossible—impossible ! We believed in him so. And my guardian ! What will he think—what will he do ? Are you sure it's true ?

RODERICK WENALLT : I've given you the facts. You must put your own construction upon them.

LADY VIOLET (*paces the room in distress, her face pale, her eyes strained ; pausing by the table, she takes up the sketch, slowly tears it up, and drops it bit by bit on the floor*) : You've surprised me—hurt me. (*She brushes past* RODERICK WENALLT, *without looking up, and hastily quits the room.*)

RODERICK WENALLT *looks after her with a gleam of triumph in his eyes. Rings bell. Lights cigarette.*

FOOTMAN *enters.*

RODERICK WENALLT : Williams, I want you

126

to tell Mr. Garth, as soon as he is disengaged, that a gentleman wishes to see him in the Library. You needn't mention any name (*tips servant*). Don't let anyone interrupt us.

FOOTMAN : Very good, sir. (*Exit.*)

RODERICK WENALLT *takes up a newspaper, and drops into an easy chair, his eyes fixed on the door. In a few moments* GARTH *comes in, and looks surprised to see* RODERICK WENALLT.

LLEWELYN GARTH : I thought you had gone.

RODERICK WENALLT : I waited to see you. I'm going to do some plain speaking.

LLEWELYN GARTH : The plainer the better.

RODERICK WENALLT : Look here, Garth—you'll have to go. You must see for yourself that things can't go on as they are !

LLEWELYN GARTH : I see that you want to get rid of me.

RODERICK WENALLT : I do.—It's you or me, and I prefer it should be you. You've ousted me from Parliament ; you've put that fool, Wilkin, in my place ; you've set Lord Wenallt against me. You've even tainted Lady Violet with your damned " ideals," and made the air of Wenallt stink with the fumes of your infernal factory.

LLEWELYN GARTH : Blame yourself for these things—not me. I've fought you with clean hands.

RODERICK WENALLT : Clean hands ! You

ruined that poor devil, Jenkin Lewis. Don't talk to me about clean hands.

LLEWELYN GARTH : Oh, no, I didn't ruin him. Unfortunately for him, he listened to you, not to me. And there's another matter—Lewis' girl (*confronting* RODERICK WENALLT.) Where is she? (*Threateningly*) I want to know, and I'll have the truth.

RODERICK WENALLT (*shrinking a little*) : My dear fellow, I thought you knew.

LLEWELYN GARTH (*restraining himself with difficulty*) : Don't try to play with me. I'll have the truth—now. (RODERICK WENALLT *stands further away, half-sneering, half-afraid—silent—warily watching* GARTH.) If you won't tell me— (*takes a swift step towards* RODERICK WENALLT)— by God ! I'll shake the truth out of you.

RODERICK WENALLT : I really thought you knew. I did, indeed. I'm quite willing to admit that I took her away.

LLEWELYN GARTH : You admit it !

RODERICK WENALLT : Oh, yes, between ourselves. She came with me willingly enough. But the little fool took fright, and gave me the slip at Oxford. I've not seen her since. It was quite a harmless flight—so far as she was concerned.

LLEWELYN GARTH : I'm glad to hear that. It's fortunate for you.

RODERICK WENALLT : Extenuating circumstances—what ? The queer thing is that *you* are suspected of enticing the girl away.

LLEWELYN GARTH : I am suspected ? Is this another lie ?

RODERICK WENALLT : It's a delightful bit of irony, isn't it ? The villain goes free, and the hero is pilloried. Even Lady Violet suspects you.

LLEWELYN GARTH : I don't believe it.

RODERICK WENALLT (*shrugs his shoulders*) : As you like. Evidence is stronger than sentiment. It almost convinced me. Presents of £10 notes to a girl, and that sort of thing, play the devil with one's respectability.

LLEWELYN GARTH (*uneasily*) : I see, you've made up a pretty story.

RODERICK WENALLT *picks up torn sketch— pieces it together—hands it to* GARTH.

LLEWELYN GARTH (*staring at it*) : What's this ?

RODERICK WENALLT : A shattered idol. It's you—drawn and torn up by the same hand—Lady Violet's.

LLEWELYN GARTH : Then you have told her this infamous lie ?

RODERICK WENALLT : I answered her questions. She drew her own conclusions. A woman can always convince herself of anything she wishes

129

to believe. The ten pound note was the turning point in the game—it did for you.

LLEWELYN GARTH (*agitated*) : I will see her at once (*moves quickly towards door*).

RODERICK WENALLT : I wouldn't, if I were you. (GARTH *hesitates.*) There's something else—a greater barrier between you than Arlais Lewis.

LLEWELYN GARTH : I suppose this is a jest ?

RODERICK WENALLT : Oh, no—it's a little family secret that has come to light—just at the right time.

LLEWELYN GARTH : Will you speak plainly ?

RODERICK WENALLT : Delighted, I'm sure. (*laughs cynically*). You have the honour to be Lord Wenallt's son.

LLEWELYN GARTH (*incredulously*) : Lord Wenallt's son ?

RODERICK WENALLT : I beg your pardon ! I should have said his " natural son." (GARTH *stares at him—startled—bewildered*) : It does make a lot of difference, doesn't it ? Let us call it an episode in the secret history of a Cabinet Minister. It sounds better, and won't shock the sensitive ears of Lady Violet so much perhaps as the cruder formula.

LLEWELYN GARTH : If you are lying to me !—Take care !

RODERICK WENALLT : Oh, no. I'm not quite such a fool. Do you think Lord Wenallt would have

130

done so much for you, spent tons of money on your fancy schemes, if you had been nothing nearer to him than a promising young man of ideas ? Think for a moment, and let your reason have a chance.

LLEWELYN GATRH (*staggered*) : I can't believe it.—My God ! if it's true, what am I ?

RODERICK WENALLT : It is rough on you.— What'll you do ?

GARTH *turns away from him, his face white and drawn, like a man staggering under an overwhelming blow.*

RODERICK WENALLT (*watches him, and the sneer dies out of his face*) : Oh, look here, Garth, don't take it so much to heart. The world is wide, and there are plenty of adventures for the man who seeks them.

LLEWELYN GARTH (*to himself*) : I must see Lord Wenallt at once. (*Gropes his way in blind distress towards the door—pauses to recover himself, his hand on the handle of the door.*)

RODERICK WENALLT (*uneasily*) : I wouldn't see him just yet, if I were you. You are looking devilish bad, you know, and it might give the dear old boy a shock. Conscience, and all that. (GARTH *wavers, turns from the door.*) Pull yourself together, man.

LLEWELYN GARTH (*walks slowly round the room—his eyes fixed on the floor*) : You've struck me

131

harder than you know. All I lived for has fallen away from me. Someone might have told me—surely, my—Lord Wenallt might have warned me, and not let me drift into such a position. A fool's paradise, and now—disaster ! (*he continues his walk, with bent head, silently, deeply thinking, watched by* RODERICK WENALLT). It means beginning all over again—(*raise his head, and glances suddenly at* RODERICK WENALLT)—but I'll do it. You have dragged me down, but the end is not yet—not yet !

RODERICK WENALLT (*with reluctant admiration*) : It's a thousand pities you were born on the wrong side of the hedge, Garth. The " bar sinister " does make such a devil of a lot of difference. What are you going to do ? You'll not stay here, of course?

LLEWELYN GARTH : What I do doesn't concern you.

RODERICK WENALLT : Oh, I don't know. I'd like to help you. Look here—if you'll clear out at once, I'll take over your duties until Lord Wenallt finds a new secretary.

LLEWELYN GARTH : I must see Lord Wenallt.

RODERICK WENALLT : Oh, if you are bent on it, you must do as you like. But it'll be devilish unpleasant for you.

LLEWELYN GARTH : That doesn't matter—I'll see him.

RODERICK WENALLT : Well, I am damned !

LORD WENALLT *enters hurriedly, and crosses to the desk.*

LORD WENALLT : I left some notes here.——Ah ! here they are (*picks up notes, glances at them, raises his head, sees* RODERICK WENALLT). Hullo, Roderick, come over for the demonstration ?

RODERICK WENALLT : Yes. I thought I'd just show myself to——(*with a laugh*)——the rabble.

LORD WENALLT : That's right. Only don't call the people " rabble." We are all children of Adam, remember, in spite of the fences we've raised to mark off the classes in separate pens.

LLEWELYN GARTH (*with white, set face*) : My lord, may I see you a moment, privately ?

LORD WENALLT (*hurriedly*) : Not now——not now ! I haven't a moment to spare. (*Goes hastily to the balcony——looks out——returns quickly*) : The people are gathering rapidly. We must hurry up (*fails to notice* GARTH'S *agitation*).

RODERICK WENALLT *withdraws to the far end of the room, and watches the scene with intense satisfaction.*)

LLEWELYN GARTH (*earnestly——appealingly*) : But, my lord——

LORD WENALLT : Don't " my lord " me, Garth.

LLEWELYN GARTH (*starts*) : It is urgent. I——I——must speak to you——just a few minutes.

133

LORD WENALLT : Speak to me to-morrow. To-morrow shall be yours. It is impossible now.

LLEWELYN GARTH (*places himself in front of* LORD WENALLT, *who notices the lines of sharp suffering in* GARTH'S *face*) : You must hear me—you must—(*passionately*)—you must !

LORD WENALLT (*with an appealing gesture*) : Please !——

There is a pause. LORD WENALLT *is much moved—he glances uneasily two or three times at* GARTH, *and seems on the point of speaking, but keeps silent.*

LLEWELYN GARTH (*desperately—in a low, intense voice, fixing haggard eyes upon* LORD WENALLT) : Who am I ?—What am I ? (*Sways a little —clutches at the back of a chair with nervous, working fingers—waiting in strained expectation for* LORD WENALLT'S *answer*) : I demand to know. I—I have a right to know.

LORD WENALLT : Ha ! (*glances sharply over to* RODERICK WENALLT) : So, that is it ! (*Another pause—very kindly to* GARTH) Ring the bell, my boy.

GARTH, *too overcome to move from the chair, stammers something—sweeps his hand slowly across his forehead—drops into a seat.* LORD WENALLT *moves to* GARTH, *lays a hand on his arm, nods encouragingly, crosses to the bell, and rings.*

The crowd cheers outside. WILKIN *beckons to* LORD WENALLT *from the balcony.* DAVIE *is in attendance.*

FOOTMAN *enters, and stands by the door.*

LORD WENALLT : Ask her ladyship to be good enough to come here, Williams.

FOOTMAN : Yes, my lord. (*Exit.*)

LORD WENALLT (*to* GARTH) : Wait, my boy, wait !

The crowd again cheers, and WILKIN *flourishes his hands to the crowd, then trots in, with* DAVIE *at his heels.*

WILKIN WATKINS : Come on, my lord ! The people are wanting you. They'll eat you—(*chuckles*)—if you don't go quick.

LORD WENALLT (*to* GARTH) : I must speak to them.

*Crowd cheering—*LORD WENALLT, WILKIN, *and* DAVIE *step out on to the balcony, and disappear.*

LADY WENALLT *comes in in earnest conversation with* JACOB MORGAN. RODERICK WENALLT *keeps out of sight.* GARTH *rests his head on his hands in an attitude of despondency, too overcome by his trouble to notice* LADY WENALLT, *until she lays her hand gently upon his head.*

LADY WENALLT : Garth !

LLEWELYN GARTH (*looks up*) : Lady Wenallt ! (*stands up*).

THE GREAT EXPERIMENT

LADY WENALLT : Dear boy ! What's the matter ? Tell me ? (GARTH *shakes his head— tries to smile.*) You can't deceive me (*looks round quickly—anxiously*). Where is your father—Oh ! What have I said !

LLEWELYN GARTH : It is true then ! (GARTH'S *head droops again—in utter misery.*)

LADY WENALLT (*distressed*) : No—yes—Oh ! I don't know what I'm saying.

LLEWELYN GARTH : That is all I wanted to know (*moving slowly to the door*). I have no right to be here. Every moment I remain is an insult to Lady Violet.

LADY WENALLT (*wildly*) : Garth ! don't talk that. I don't know what you mean (*he is near the door, his hand resting on it.*) (*Imploringly*) : Come back—come back ! It is all wrong !

LLEWELYN GARTH (*sadly*) : Yes—it is all wrong—bitterly wrong.

LADY WENALLT (*pleadingly*) : You will break my heart—if you go now. You don't know—(*breaks off—looks towards balcony*). Oh ! why doesn't Wen come !

LLEWELYN GARTH : I am sorry you are so distressed, Lady Wenallt. But—don't worry about me. If you wish me to see Lord Wenallt I will wait—because *you* ask me—but—but I would rather not.

LADY WENALLT : Thank you, Garth. I knew

136

you wouldn't disappoint me. I have much to tell you that I long to tell you, but your—Lord Wenallt made me promise to wait until he is present. I trust him, Garth, and you must trust him, too.

LLEWELYN GARTH (*bows gravely*): I will try —as you wish it.

LORD WENALLT, WILKIN, *and* DAVIE, *reappear on the balcony.*

LADY WENALLT: Here he is—at last ! (*She hurries to* LORD WENALLT, *who comes to meet her, and whispers to him earnestly. He nods and smiles.*

While this is taking place WILKIN *trots into the the room, with* DAVIE.

WILKIN WATKINS: Morning, Jacob.

JACOB MORGAN: Glad to see you, Mr. Watkins.

WILKIN WATKINS: I am glad to see myself, too, when I am not in trouble (*chuckles*).

DAVIE *helps* WILKIN *off with his coat, takes his hat, and carries them out.*

LORD WENALLT (*with one foot in the room, the other on the step leading to the balcony*): Only a few minutes, dear one. Where is Violet ?

LADY WENALLT: With a friend. She will be here in a moment.

The cheering outside breaks out afresh, and grows louder. LORD WENALLT *steps out on to the balcony, taking* LADY WENALLT *with him, and receives a great ovation.*

137

THE GREAT EXPERIMENT

LORD WENALLT (*addresses the crowd in the grounds—from the balcony*) : My friends ! Welcome once more to Wenallt. I am pleased to see so many familiar faces before me. It shows that time has not severed the links of friendship which the years have forged between us (*cheers*). Gentlemen ! we have been passing through critical times. The war has left its mark upon us. It has shown us how all classes can work together for the common good. The Empire has been reconsecrated by the blood of her sons. Political enmities have been obliterated by the glorious renascence of the national spirit. Politicians have placed their country before their Party and their conscience before their ambition. The best elements of all Parties have joined forces in the interests of the State. The country has never been so well governed. After such an experience, shall we go back to the old vicious system ? (*Loud cries—" No, no, never !"*) From my soul I say with you—" Never !" No ! Let us have none of the old hatreds revived. Let our cry be—Co-operation, Unity, Peace ! And recollect, Peace between Nations can only be founded on racial rights ; and peace in the industrial world only on a basis of mutual interests. (*Great cheering.*)

LORD WENALLT'S *speech gradually rouses* GARTH *out of himself. Unconsciously he is drawn towards the balcony, and* LADY WENALLT *leaves* LORD

138

WENALLT'S *side and joins* GARTH—*speaks to him
eagerly and leads him aside. At first he listens
sombrely. Gradually an expression of amazement,
then of unspeakable relief, spreads over his face. He
raises* LADY WENALLT'S *hand impulsively to his
lips, and kisses it almost passionately. He looks
across at* RODERICK WENALLT, *who is watching him
with a puzzled frown, and a shadow passes swiftly
across his countenance.* JACOB MORGAN *smiles and
chats with* WILKIN, *who frequently looks across at*
RODERICK WENALLT.

LADY WENALLT : Listen, Garth. You will
understand everything very soon.

GARTH *links his arm in* LADY WENALLT'S, *and
leads her to the window, where they stand together,
listening and whispering eagerly.*

RODERICK WENALLT *watches their movements
with growing curiosity and uneasiness.*

LORD WENALLT : We in this Village have been
pioneers in the practical application of Co-operation.
You see it at work in our New Factory. Shall I call
it Garth's Factory ? (*Loud cries—" Garth's Factory
—bravo, Garth !"*) The credit for what has been
achieved is due to him. His knowledge of your needs,
your hopes and fears, gleaned in a hard school, he
brought to me, to be sifted and considered and applied
as you have seen it applied in our midst. (*Three
cheers given for* GARTH *by the crowd.*) Here, we

don't have the rich battling with the poor ; the employer fighting the workman ; the politician promising remedies for to-morrow——(WILKIN *and* JACOB MORGAN *turn their eyes upon* RODERICK WENALLT, *and nod significantly)*——with hell on earth to-day ; the cold and hungry starving, while Sects and Parties revile each other and fight for Self. Shall we go back to the old days ?

WILKIN WATKINS (*rushes on to the balcony*) : Never, boys, never ! The old days are as dead as mutton, ain't they, Davie ? (*looks round for* DAVIE.) Oh, Davie isn't here. Never mind. He is a bit of old-times, too, so we don't want him. You are very wise people in the village. (*Laughter.*) ("*Good old Wilkin.*") I tell you you are. Didn't you send me to Parliament ? (*Laughter.*) Very well then. Wise people can't do a foolish thing, and go back to the rotten old times, when you had as much darns as cloth on your back, and your Member——(*slaps his chest*)——slept in a kennel (*chuckles and retires*). (LORD WENALLT *laughingly claps him on the back.*)

LADY WENALLT (*takes* GARTH'S *arm*) : Come, my dear son——(RODERICK WENALLT *jumps to his feet—seems dumbfounded*)——and speak to your friends. This is your hour—and mine.—— Come !

GARTH *follows* LADY WENALLT *reluctantly on to*

140

the balcony. LORD WENALLT *turns to* GARTH *with outstretched hands.*

LORD WENALLT : Your mother has told you ? I see she has (*they grasp hands*).

GARTH *stands on the balcony between* LORD *and* LADY WENALLT.

LORD WENALLT : Gentlemen ! You know Mr. Garth as your very good friend (*takes* GARTH'S *arm and leads him forward to the rail*). Now know him as my son.

RODERICK WENALLT (*to himself*) : What infernal luck ! (*throws himself into a chair*).

The crowd. having got over their surprise, cheer wildly. During the cheering, LADY VIOLET *and* ARLAIS LEWIS *enter, smiling and chatting.* RODERICK WENALLT, *taken aback at the sight of* ARLAIS LEWIS, *quickly recovers himself, and hastens towards* LADY VIOLET *and* ARLAIS. *They stand still and cold as he approaches, and then deliberately turn their backs upon him, leaving him face to face with* JENKIN LEWIS, *who has followed them into the room.*

JENKIN LEWIS (*his face darkening, his eyes flashing, lifts his stick threatiningly*) : You blackguard ! It was you—you ! and you put the fault on Garth. The world shall know what you are.

ARLAIS LEWIS : Father ! (*drags her father away.*)

LADY VIOLET, ARLAIS, JENKIN LEWIS, JACOB

MORGAN, *and* WILKIN *gather together, and whisper eagerly.* LADY VIOLET *rests her hand on* JACOB MORGAN'S *arm, and her eyes dwell upon his face affectionately. As soon as* GARTH *begins to speak* LADY VIOLET *steals to the window, and listens to him with a smiling, happy face.*

LLEWELYN GARTH (*facing the crowd*): What shall I say to you? At a moment like this I feel too much to be able to talk or think. I have been found, it's true; but I feel more lost than ever (*laughter from the crowd.*) To-morrow I will come amongst you. Until then, thank you all for coming to greet me in the presence of my father and mother.

LORD WENALLT: Bravo! Bravo! Garth.

GARTH *waves his hand and bows to the crowd.*

WILKIN WATKINS (*tosses cigarette case to* RODERICK WENALLT): Yours, Mr. Wenallt. Me and Davie found it in Jenkin Lewis' shop the night you run away with Miss Arlais, and she run away from you at Oxford (*chuckles.*)

LLEWELYN GARTH (*turns from the crowd, sees* LADY VIOLET *and* ARLAIS—*surprised*): Lady Violet! Arlais!

LADY VIOLET *hangs back nervously.* ARLAIS *hurries forward, and grasps* GARTH'S *hand.*

ARLAIS LEWIS (*nods and smiles at* LADY VIOLET): She knows, Garth.

LLEWELYN GARTH (*crosses to* LADY VIOLET):

Lady—Violet, am I forgiven for the things I didn't do?

LADY VIOLET (*looking down nervously*) : It is I who need forgiveness—Lord Garth.

LLEWELYN GARTH : *Lord* Garth?

LADY VIOLET : Is it an unpleasant surprise—Garth?

LLEWELYN GARTH (*intensely happy*) : Dreadfully unpleasant, from your lips. I shall want to be just " Garth " to you all my life.

He quickly leads LADY VIOLET *on to the balcony, draws her arm through his. They stand there, smiling and bowing, and the crowd cheer frantically.*

CURTAIN.

CARDIFF :

THE EDUCATIONAL PUBLISHING CO., LTD.